CW01647561

M

Roman Transliteration of

Part 29

OF THE HOLY QUR'AN

With Arabic Text

English Translation
By 'Abdullah Yusuf' Ali
Edited in Modern Standard English

DAR AL TAQWA LTD
دار التقوى

Dar Al Taqwa Ltd. 1998

Part 29 of the Holy Quran

ISBN 1-870582-11-X

Cover Design by Ahmed Nigm

Republished by:
Dar Al Taqwa Ltd.
7A, Melcombe Street
Baker Street
London
NW1 6AE
email: dar.altaqwa@btinternet.com

Printed and Bound by- De-Luxe Printers,
London NW10 7NR.
website: http://www.de-luxe.com
email: printers@de-luxe.com

Table of Contents

In the Name of God the Most
Merciful the Most Compassionate

In the Name of Allah
the Merciful, the Compassionate

Introduction

Praise be to Allah (may He be exalted), Who bestowed His Blessings upon us. He is the One Who guided us to Islam , the straight path.. We pray to the Almighty to shower His blessings and peace upon our beloved Prophet, Muhammad ibn `Abd Allah. We hereby testify that he has conveyed the message to us, and gave mankind the best example of the human character to emulate.

This booklet represents an effort by some concerned Muslims to help English-speaking Muslims to learn the recitation the *Surahs* of the 29th. Part of the Qur'an. It is a continuation of an earlier good work that started in 1979 by Br. Ibrahim El Dosougi Mohammad when he introduced Part 30 of the Qur'an in transliterated format. That work was well received and appreciated by many brothers and sisters who used it either to learn or to teach the recitation of the Qur'an.

The need to bring more parts of the Qur'an in this format is growing. It is an obligation upon those who know the language of the Qur'an to make it accessible for others by teaching them to learn the recitation of the Qur'an in Arabic. If classes to teach Arabic are not available; a transliteration becomes very helpful to make Qur'anic text accessible to whoever desires it.

When one transliterates the glorious Qur'an the question arises : Why should the Qur'anic text be printed in Roman Alphabet? It may also be argued that this kind of work could become a hindrance to the learning of the language of the Qur'an by new Muslims. And when we add to these observations the practical academic difficulties in presenting Arabic Language characters and sounds in another alphabet. These are relevant questions and observations which deserve to be addressed by the concerned workers for *da`wah* among non-Arabic peoples .

It is required from Muslims to recite the Qur'an and work on understanding its message. The mere recitation of the Qur'an in itself is highly recommended as an act of worship that will bring the individual a lot of rewards. The prophet Muhammad (may Allah's peace and blessings be showered upon him) has told us that whoever recites the Qur'an (or even tries with difficulties to do so) will be rewarded by Allah ten *hasanat* (rewards) for each letter recited, and Allah may multiply His rewards up to seven hundred times and more to whomever He wills.

By the grace of Allah, Islam is spreading in a pace faster than the ability of Muslim organizations to meet the needs of new Muslims. It becomes a matter of necessity to help the new converts or (reverts) - who do not know Arabic - to train themselves in the recitation of the Qur'an. Printing the Qur'anic text in the transliterated format becomes a practical means of acquainting them with the language of the Qur'an.

There are few suggestions for the prospected users of this, booklet to help them benefit from it :

a- To look for someone who speaks Arabic to train the user in getting to recognize and pronounce the Arabic characters.

b- If there is no one - who speaks Arabic- available, it is commended to use the educational version of the Qur'anic recitation tapes to listen to them and try to emulate the recitation .

c- To get to know the rules of the transliteration system which has been adopted in this work.

Furthermore we chose to adopt the translation of the meaning of the Qur'an of `Abd Allah Yusuf `Ali which is considered by many as one of the best translations available in English. We tried to update its language to modern standard English to benefit of contemporary readers.

I wish here to express my appreciation to:

Al Saa`dawi Publications for encouraging me to do this work . I pray to Allah *subhanahu wa ta`ala* to reward all those who work to make the words of Allah (the Qur'an) accessible to those who seek guidance .

`Ali R. Abuza`kuk

Burke, VA

July 1995

Key to Transliteration

The rules that govern the transliteration system we have adopted in this work are based upon the phonetic system. We consulted the system suggested by the late Professor Isma`il al Faruqi in his book *Toward Islamic English.* We also consulted and benefitted from the system of the Library of Congress. The Arabic Alphabet letters are represented as follows:

Letter	Translit.	Arabic
hamzah	‘ (apostrophe)	Á
alif	a	Ç
ba'	b	È
ta'	t	Ê
tha'	th as in bath	Ë
jim	j	Ì
ha'	h	Í
kha'	kh	Î
dal	d	Ï
dhal	dh as in thee	Ð
ra'	r	Ñ
za'	z	Ò
sin	s as in sir	Ó
shin	sh as ship	Ô
sad	s	Õ

dad	d	Ö
`ayn	` (inverted apostrphe)	Ú
<u>gh</u>ayn	<u>gh</u>	Û
fa'	f	Ý
qaf	*q*	Þ
kaf	k	ß
lam	l	á
mim	m	ã
nun	n	ä
ha'	h	åÜ
waw	w	æ
ya'	y	í

- The diphtongs are transcribed as (aw Çæ) and (ay Çì)
- Regular long vowels are indicated by two consecutive vowels: as in aa, uu, and ii.
- Vowels elongated by the *maddah* ~ are indicated by an additional vowel as in *Laaa uqsimu bi -yawmil- qiyaamah* áÂ ÃÞÓã Èíæã ÇáÞíÇãÉ

سُورَةُ المُلك

Al Mulk

جزء 29

Bismillaahir - Rahmaanir - Rahiim. بسم الله الرحمن الرحيم

1. Tabaarakalladhi bi-Yadihil - MULK; wa Huwa 'alaa kulli shay - 'in - Qadeer:-

١- تبارك الذي بيده الملك
وهو على كل شيء قدير

2. Alladhi khalaqal - Mawta wal-Hayaata li - yabluwakum ayyu-kum ahsanu 'amalan: wa Hu-wal - 'Aziizul - Gafur; -

٢- الذي خلق الموت والحيوة
ليبلوكم أيكم أحسن عملا
وهو العزيز الغفور

3. 'Alladhi khalaqa sab'a samaawaatin - tibaaqan: maa taraa fi Khalqir - Rahmanni min-tafaa-wut. Farji-'il-basara hal taraa min-futuur ?

٣- الذي خلق سبع سموت طباقا
ما ترى في خلق الرحمن من
تفوت فارجع البصر
هل ترى من فطور

In the name of Allah, Most Gracious, Most Merciful.

1. Blessed is He In Whose Hands is Dominion: And He over all things Has Power;

2. He Who created Death And Life, that He May try which of you is best in deed: And He is the Exalted in Might, Oft-Forgiving; -

3. He Who created the seven heavens One above another; No want of proportion will you see in the Creation of (Allah) Most Gracious So turn your vision again: You will not See any flaw ?

4. Thummar-ji-'il-basara kar-
ratayni yanqalib 'ilaykal-basaru
khaashi-'an -wa huwa hasiir.

٤- ثُمَّ ارْجِعِ الْبَصَرَ كَرَّتَيْنِ
يَنْقَلِبْ إِلَيْكَ الْبَصَرُ خَاسِئًا
وَهُوَ حَسِيرٌ ○

5. Wa laqad zayyannas-samaa-
addunya bimasaabiha wa
ja-'alnaaha rujuumal - lish-
shayaatini wa a'tadna la-
hum 'adhaabas-Sa-`iir.

٥- وَلَقَدْ زَيَّنَّا السَّمَاءَ الدُّنْيَا
بِمَصَابِيحَ
وَجَعَلْنَاهَا رُجُومًا لِّلشَّيَاطِينِ
وَأَعْتَدْنَا لَهُمْ
عَذَابَ السَّعِيرِ ○

6. Wa liilladhina kafaruu bi-
Rabbihim 'dhaabu Jahannama:
wa bi'-sal-masiir.

٦- وَلِلَّذِينَ كَفَرُوا بِرَبِّهِمْ
عَذَابُ جَهَنَّمَ وَبِئْسَ الْمَصِيرُ ○

4. Again turn your vision a second time; (your) vision will come back to you Dull and discomfited, in a state worn out.

5. And We have, (From of old), Adorned the lowest heaven with Lamps and We Have made such (Lamps), (as) missiles to drive away the Evil Ones, And have prepared for them the Penalty Of the Blazing Fire

6. For those who reject Their Lord (and Cherisher) Is the Penalty of Hell: And evil is (such) destination.

7. Idha ulquu fiihaa sami-'uu laha shahiiqanw-wa hiya tafuur, -

٧- إِذَآ أُلْقُوا فِيهَا سَمِعُوا
لَهَا شَهِيقًا وَّهِيَ تَفُورُ ۝

8. Takaadu tamayyazu minal-ghayz: kullamaaa 'ulqiya fiihaa fawjun sa-'alahum khazanatu-haaa 'alam ya'-tikum Nadhiir ?

٨- تَكَادُ تَمَيَّزُ مِنَ الْغَيْظِ ۖ
كُلَّمَآ أُلْقِيَ فِيهَا فَوْجٌ سَأَلَهُمْ
خَزَنَتُهَآ أَلَمْ يَأْتِكُمْ نَذِيرٌ ۝

9. Qaaluu balaa qad jaaa-'anaa Nadhir; fakadhdhabnaa wa qulnaa maa nazzalallaahu min-shay' : 'in 'antum 'illaa fii zalaalin-kabiir !

٩- قَالُوا بَلَىٰ قَدْ جَآءَنَا نَذِيرٌ ۙ
فَكَذَّبْنَا وَقُلْنَا مَا نَزَّلَ اللَّهُ مِن
شَيْءٍ ۚ إِنْ أَنتُمْ إِلَّا فِي ضَلَٰلٍ كَبِيرٍ ۝

10. Wa qaaluu law kunnaa nasma-'u 'aw na'-qilu maa kun-naa fiii 'As-habis-Sa-'iir.

١٠- وَقَالُوا لَوْ كُنَّا نَسْمَعُ
أَوْ نَعْقِلُ مَا كُنَّا فِيٓ
أَصْحَٰبِ السَّعِيرِ ۝

7. When they are cast therein,they will hear The (terrible) drawing in of its breath Even as it blazes forth,

8. Almost bursting with fury: Every time a Group Is cast therein, its Keepers will ask, " Did no Warner come to you ? "

9. They will say: " Yes indeed: A Warner did come to us, But we rejected him and said, ' Allah never Sent down any (Message): you are nothing but an egregious delusion ! ' "

10.They will further say: " Had we but listened Or used our intelligence, we should not (now) Be among the Companions of the Blazing Fire ! "

11. Fa'-tarafuu bi-dhambihim :
fasuh-qal-li As-haabis-Sa-'iir !

١١- فَاعْتَرَفُوا بِذَنْۢبِهِمْ ۚ
فَسُحْقًا لِّأَصْحٰبِ السَّعِيْرِ ۝

12. 'Innalladhiina yakh-shawna
Rabbahum - bil-ghaybi lahum-
Maghfiratunw-wa 'Ajrun-kabiir.

١٢- إِنَّ الَّذِيْنَ يَخْشَوْنَ رَبَّهُمْ بِالْغَيْبِ
لَهُمْ مَّغْفِرَةٌ وَّأَجْرٌ كَبِيْرٌ ۝

13. Wa 'asirruu qawlakum
awij-haruu bihi; innahuu
`Aliimum-bidhaatis-suduur.

١٣- وَأَسِرُّوْا قَوْلَكُمْ أَوِ اجْهَرُوْا بِهٖ ۖ
إِنَّهٗ عَلِيْمٌۢ بِذَاتِ الصُّدُوْرِ ۝

14. Alaa ya'-lamu man kha-
laqa ? Wa Huwal - Latiiful-
Khabiir. (Section 2)

١٤- أَلَا يَعْلَمُ
مَنْ خَلَقَ ۖ
وَهُوَ اللَّطِيْفُ الْخَبِيْرُ ۝

11. They will then confess their sins: but far will be (Forgiveness) From the Companions of the Blazing Fire !

12. As for those who fear their Lord unseen, For them is Forgiveness and a great Reward.

13. And whether you hide your word or publish it, He certainly has (full) knowledge, Of the secrets of (all) hearts.

14. Should He not know, He that created ? And He is the One that understands the finest Mysteries (and) is Well-acquainted (with them).

15. Huwalladhii ja-'ala lakumul-
arda dhaluulan - fa'mshuu fii
manaakibihaa wa kuluu mir-
Rizqih: wa 'ilay-hin-Nushuur.

١٥- هُوَ الَّذِىْ جَعَلَ لَكُمُ الْاَرْضَ ذَلُوْلًا
فَامْشُوْا فِىْ مَنَاكِبِهَا
وَكُلُوْا مِنْ رِّزْقِهٖ ؕ
وَاِلَيْهِ النُّشُوْرُ ۝

16. 'A - 'amintum - man -fis-
Samaaa-'i 'any-yakh-sifa bi-
kumul - 'arda fa-'idha hiya
tamuur ?

١٦- ءَاَمِنْتُمْ مَّنْ فِى السَّمَآءِ
اَنْ يَّخْسِفَ بِكُمُ الْاَرْضَ
فَاِذَا هِىَ تَمُوْرُ ۝

17. Am 'amintum-man - fis-
Samaaa-'i 'any-yursila 'alay-
kum haasibaa ? Fa sata'- lamuu-
na kayfa nadhiir.

١٧- اَمْ اَمِنْتُمْ مَّنْ فِى السَّمَآءِ
اَنْ يُّرْسِلَ عَلَيْكُمْ حَاصِبًا ؕ
فَسَتَعْلَمُوْنَ
كَيْفَ نَذِيْرِ ۝

15. It is He Who has made the earth mangageable For you, so traverse you through its tracts And enjoy of the Sustenance which He furnishes: but unto Him is the Resurrection

16. Do you feel secure that He Who is in Heaven Will not cause you to be swallowed up By the earth when it shakes (as in an earthquake) ?

17. Or do you feel secure that He Who is in Heaven Will not Send against you a violent tornado (With showers of stones), so that you shall Know how (terrible) was My warning?

18. Wa laqad kadhdhaba-llidhiina
min-qablihim fa-kay-fa kaana
nakiir ?

١٨- وَلَقَدْ كَذَّبَ الَّذِينَ مِنْ قَبْلِهِمْ
فَكَيْفَ كَانَ نَكِيرِ ۝

19. 'Awalam yaraw 'ilat-tayri
fawqahum saaaffaatinw-wa
yaq-bidn ? Maa yumsiku-
hunna 'illar-Rahmaan:
'innahuu bi-kulli shay - 'im-
Basiir.

١٩- أَوَلَمْ يَرَوْا إِلَى الطَّيْرِ فَوْقَهُمْ
صَٰٓفَّٰتٍ وَيَقْبِضْنَ ۚ
مَا يُمْسِكُهُنَّ إِلَّا الرَّحْمَٰنُ ۚ
إِنَّهُۥ بِكُلِّ شَيْءٍۭ بَصِيرٌ ۝

20. 'Amman haadhalladhii huwa
jundul-lakum yansurukum-min
duunir-Rahmaan ? 'Inil-kaafi-
ruuna 'illaa fii ghuruur.

٢٠- أَمَّنْ هَٰذَا الَّذِي هُوَ جُندٌ لَّكُمْ
يَنصُرُكُم مِّن دُونِ الرَّحْمَٰنِ ۚ
إِنِ الْكَٰفِرُونَ إِلَّا فِي غُرُورٍ ۝

18. But indeed men before them rejected (My warning): Then how (terrible) was My rejection (of them)

19. Do they not observe the birds above them. Spreading their wings and folding them in ? None can uphold them except (Allah) Most Gracious: Truly it is He That wathches over all things.

20. Nay, who is there that can help you, (Even as) an army, besides (Allah) Most Merciful ? In nothing but delusion are the unbelievers.

21. 'Amman haadhalladhii yar-
zuqukum 'in 'amsaka Rizqah ?
Bal-lajjuu fii 'utuwwinw-wa
nufuur.

٢١-أَمَّنْ هَٰذَا الَّذِي يَرْزُقُكُمْ
إِنْ أَمْسَكَ رِزْقَهُ ۚ
بَل لَّجُّوا فِي عُتُوٍّ وَنُفُورٍ ○

22. 'Afamany-yamshii mukib-
ban 'alaa wajhihiii 'ahdaaa 'am-
many-yamshii sa-wiyyan 'alaa
Siraatim-Mustaqiim.

٢٢-أَفَمَن يَمْشِي مُكِبًّا عَلَىٰ وَجْهِهِ
أَهْدَىٰ أَمَّن يَمْشِي سَوِيًّا
عَلَىٰ صِرَاطٍ مُّسْتَقِيمٍ ○

23. Qul Huwalladhiii 'ansha-
'akum wa ja-'ala lakums-
sam-'a wal-'absaara wal-'af-
'idah: qaliilam-maa tash-ku
ruun.

٢٣-قُلْ هُوَ الَّذِي أَنشَأَكُمْ
وَجَعَلَ لَكُمُ
السَّمْعَ وَالْأَبْصَارَ وَالْأَفْئِدَةَ ۖ
قَلِيلًا مَّا تَشْكُرُونَ ○

24. Qul Huwalladhii dhara-'akum
fil-'ardi wa 'ilay-hi tuh-sharuun.

٢٤-قُلْ هُوَ الَّذِي ذَرَأَكُمْ
فِي الْأَرْضِ وَإِلَيْهِ تُحْشَرُونَ ○

21. Or who is there that can provide you With sustenance if Hewere to withhold His provision ? Nay, they obstinately persist in insolent impiety And flight (from the Truth).

22. Is then one who walks headlong, with his face grovelling, better guided, or one who walks evenly on a Straight Way ?

23. Say: " It is He Who has created you (and made you grow), and made for you the faculties of hearing, seeing, Feeling and understanding: Little thanks it is you give. "

24. Say: " It is He Who has multiplied you Through the earth, and to Him shall you Be gathered together. "

25. Wa yaquuluuna mataa haa-dh'al-wa'-du 'in - kuntum saadi-qiin.

٢٥-وَيَقُوْلُوْنَ مَتٰى هٰذَا الْوَعْدُ
اِنْ كُنْتُمْ صٰدِقِيْنَ ○

26. Qul 'innamal-'ilmu 'indal-laah: wa 'innamaaa'ana Nadhii-rum-mubiin.

٢٦-قُلْ اِنَّمَا الْعِلْمُ عِنْدَ اللّٰهِ
وَاِنَّمَآ اَنَا نَذِيْرٌ مُّبِيْنٌ ○

27. Falammaa ra-'awhu zul-fatan - siii-'at wujuuhulladhiina kafaruu wa qiila haadhalladhii kuntum-bihii tadda-'uun !

٢٧-فَلَمَّا رَاَوْهُ زُلْفَةً
سِيْٓـَٔتْ وُجُوْهُ الَّذِيْنَ كَفَرُوْا
وَقِيْلَ هٰذَا الَّذِيْ
كُنْتُمْ بِهٖ تَدَّعُوْنَ ○

25. They ask: When will this promise be (fulfilled) ? If you are telling the truth.

26. Say: " As to the knowledge of the time, it is with Allah alone: I am (sent) only to warn plainly in public. "

27. At length, when they see it close at hand, Grieved will be the faces of the Unbelievers, And it will be said (to them): " This is (the promise fulfilled),which you are calling for ! "

28. Qul 'ara-'aytum 'in 'ah-lakani - yallaahu wa mamma-'iya 'aw rahimanaa famany-yujiirul-kaafiriina min 'A<u>dh</u>aa-bin 'aliim.

٢٨- قُلْ أَرَءَيْتُمْ
إِنْ أَهْلَكَنِيَ اللّٰهُ وَمَنْ مَّعِيَ
أَوْ رَحِمَنَا
فَمَنْ يُّجِيرُ
الْكٰفِرِينَ مِنْ عَذَابٍ أَلِيمٍ ○

29. Qul Huwarl-Rahmaanu 'aa-mannaa bihii wa 'alay-hi ta-wakkal-naa: fa sata'-lamuuna man huwa fii zalaalim-mubiin.

٢٩- قُلْ هُوَ الرَّحْمٰنُ اٰمَنَّا بِهِ
وَعَلَيْهِ تَوَكَّلْنَا
فَسَتَعْلَمُونَ
مَنْ هُوَ فِي ضَلٰلٍ مُّبِينٍ ○

30. Qul 'ara-'aytum 'in 'asbaha maaa-'ukum <u>gh</u>aw-ran famany-ya'- tiikum - bi-maaa - 'im-ma-'iin ?

٣٠- قُلْ أَرَءَيْتُمْ
إِنْ أَصْبَحَ مَآؤُكُمْ غَوْرًا
فَمَنْ يَّأْتِيكُمْ بِمَآءٍ مَّعِينٍ ○ ع

28. Say: " See you ? If Allah were to destroy me, And those with me, or if he bestows His mercy on us, yet who can deliver The unbelievers from a grievous Penalty ? "

29. Say: " He is (Allah) Most Gracious: we have believed in Him, And on Him have we put our trust: So soon will you know which (of us) it is That is in manifest error."

30. Say: " can you consider? If your stream be Some morning lost (In the underground earth) Who then can supply you with clear-flowing water ?

سُورَةُ القَلَم

Al Qalam

جزء 29

Bismillaahir - Rahmaanir - Rahiim. بِسْمِ اللّٰهِ الرَّحْمٰنِ الرَّحِيْمِ

1. NUUUN. WAL-QALAMI wa maa yasturuun, -

١- نٓ وَالْقَلَمِ وَمَا يَسْطُرُوْنَ ۝

2. Maaa 'anta bi-ni'-mati Rab-bika bi-majnuun.

٢- مَآ اَنْتَ بِنِعْمَةِ رَبِّكَ بِمَجْنُوْنٍ ۝

3. Wa 'inna laka la-'Ajran ghayra mamnuun:

٣- وَاِنَّ لَكَ لَاَجْرًا غَيْرَ مَمْنُوْنٍ ۝

4. Wa 'innaka la-'alaa khulu-qın 'aziim.

٤- وَاِنَّكَ لَعَلٰى خُلُقٍ عَظِيْمٍ ۝

5. Fa satubsiru wa yubsiruun,

٥- فَسَتُبْصِرُ وَيُبْصِرُوْنَ ۝

6. Bi-'ayyikumul-maftuun.

٦- بِاَيِّيكُمُ الْمَفْتُوْنُ ۝

In the name of Allah, Most Gracious, Most Merciful.

1. *Nun.* By the Pen and by the (Record) Which (men) write,

2. You art not, by the grace of your Lord,
Mad or possessed,

3. Nay, verily for you is a Reward unfailing:

4. And you (stand) on an exalted standard Of character.

5. Soon will you see and thay will see,

6. Which of you is afflicted with madness.

7. 'Inna Rabbaka Huwa 'a'-lamu biman zalla 'an Sabiilih : wa Huwa 'A'-lamu bil-Muhtadiin.

٧-إِنَّ رَبَّكَ هُوَ أَعْلَمُ بِمَنْ ضَلَّ عَنْ سَبِيلِهِ وَهُوَ أَعْلَمُ بِالْمُهْتَدِينَ ○

8. Fa laa tuti-'il-mukadhdhibiin.

٨-فَلَا تُطِعِ الْمُكَذِّبِينَ ○

9. Wadduu law tudhinu fayudhinuun.

٩-وَدُّوا لَوْ تُدْهِنُ فَيُدْهِنُونَ ○

10. Wa laa tuti' kulla hallaafim-mahiin,

١٠-وَلَا تُطِعْ كُلَّ حَلَّافٍ مَّهِينٍ ○

11. Hammaazim-mash-shaaa-'im-binamiim,

١١-هَمَّازٍ مَّشَّاءٍ بِنَمِيمٍ ○

12. Mannaa-'il-lil-khayri mu'-tadin 'athiim,

١٢-مَّنَّاعٍ لِّلْخَيْرِ مُعْتَدٍ أَثِيمٍ ○

7. Verily it is your Lord that knows best, Which (among men) has strayed from His Path: And He knows best those who receive (True) Guidance.

8. So hearken not to those who Deny (the Truth).

9. Their desire is that you should be pliant; So would they be pliant

.

10. Feed not the type of despicable man, Ready with oaths,

11. A slanderer, going about with calumnies.

12. (Habitually) hindering (all) good Transgressing beyond bounds, deep in sin,

13. 'Utullim-ba'-da dhaalika zaniim, -

١٣- عتل بعد ذلك زنيم ۙ

14. An-kaana dhaa-maalinw-wa baniin.

١٤- ان كان ذا مال وبنين ۗ

15. Idha tut-laa 'alayhi 'Aa-yaatunaa qaala Asaatiirul-Awwaliin !

١٥- إذا تتلى عليه ايتنا
قال اساطير الاولين ۝

16. Sanasimuhuu 'alal-khur-tuum !

١٦- سنسمه على الخرطوم ۝

17. Innaa balawnaahum kamaa balawnaaa As-haabal-Jannat, 'idh 'aqsamuu layas-rimunnahaa musbihiin,

١٧- إنا بلونهم كما بلونا اصحب
الجنة
إذ اقسموا ليصرمنها مصبحين ۙ

13. Violent (and cruel), Wwth all that, base-born,

14. Because he possesses wealth and (numerous) sons,

15. When to him are rehearsed our Signs, " Tales of the Ancients ! " he cries.

16. Soon shall We brand (the beast) on the snout !

17. Verily We have tried them as We tried the People of the Garden, When they resolved to gather The fruits of the (garden) in the morning,

18. Wa laa yastath-nuun.

١٨- وَلَا يَسْتَثْنُوْنَ ○

19. Fa-taafa 'alayhaa taaa-'ifum-mir - Rabbika wa hum naaa-'imuun.

١٩- فَطَافَ عَلَيْهَا
طَآئِفٌ مِّنْ رَّبِّكَ وَهُمْ نَآئِمُوْنَ ○

20. Fa-'asbahat k'as-sariim.

٢٠- فَأَصْبَحَتْ كَالصَّرِيْمِ ○

21. Fa-tanaadaw musbihiin, -

٢١- فَتَنَادَوْا مُصْبِحِيْنَ ○

22. 'Anigh-duu 'alaa harthikum in-kuntum saarimiin.

٢٢- أَنِ اغْدُوْا عَلٰى حَرْثِكُمْ
إِنْ كُنْتُمْ صٰرِمِيْنَ ○

23. Fa'ntalaquu wa hum ya-takhaafatuun -

٢٣- فَانْطَلَقُوْا وَهُمْ يَتَخَافَتُوْنَ ○

18. But made no reservation, (" If it be Allah's Will ").

19. So there came, on the (garden) A visitation from your Lord, (Which swept away) all around, While they were asleep.

20. So the (garden) became, by the morning, like a dark and desolate spot, (Whose fruit had been gathered)

21. As the morning broke, they called out, One to another,

22. " Go you to your tilth (betimes) in morning, If you would gather the fruits. "

23. So they departed, conversing In secret low tones, (saying)

24. Allaa yad-<u>kh</u>ulannahal-yawma 'alaykum-miskiin.

٢٤- أَن لَّا يَدْخُلَنَّهَا الْيَوْمَ عَلَيْكُم مِّسْكِينٌ ۝

25. Wa <u>gh</u>adaw 'alaa hardin-qaadiriin.

٢٥- وَغَدَوْا عَلَىٰ حَرْدٍ قَادِرِينَ ۝

26. Falammaa ra-'awhaa qaaluuu'innaa ladaaalluun:

٢٦- فَلَمَّا رَأَوْهَا
قَالُوا إِنَّا لَضَالُّونَ ۝

27. Bal nahnu mahruumuun !

٢٧- بَلْ نَحْنُ مَحْرُومُونَ ۝

28. Qaala awsatuhum alam aqul-lakum law laa tusabbihuun ?

٢٨- قَالَ أَوْسَطُهُمْ
أَلَمْ أَقُل لَّكُمْ لَوْلَا تُسَبِّحُونَ ۝

29 Qaaluu 'Subhaana Rabbinaaa 'innaa kunnaa zaalimiin !

٢٩- قَالُوا سُبْحَانَ رَبِّنَا إِنَّا كُنَّا ظَالِمِينَ ۝

24. " Let not a single indigen person break in upon you into the (garden) this day. "

25. And they opened the morning, Strong in an (unjust) resolve,

26. But when they saw the (garden), they said:" We have surely lost our way:

27. " Indeed we are shut out (Of the fruits of our labor) ! "

28. Said one of them, more just (than the rest): " Did I not say to you, "'Why not glorify (Allah) ?"

29. They said: " Glory to our Lord ! Verily we have been doing wrong ! "

30. Fa-aqbala ba'-duhum 'alaa ba'-din-yatalaawamuun.

٣٠- فَأَقْبَلَ بَعْضُهُمْ عَلَىٰ بَعْضٍ يَتَلَاوَمُونَ ۝

31. Qaaluu yaa-waylanaaa innaa kunnaa taag͟hiin !

٣١- قَالُوا يَا وَيْلَنَا إِنَّا كُنَّا طَاغِينَ ۝

32. 'Asaa Rabbunaaa 'any-yubdilanaa k͟hay-ram-minhaaa 'innaaa 'ilaa Rabbinaa raag͟hibuun !

٣٢- عَسَىٰ رَبُّنَا أَنْ يُبْدِلَنَا خَيْرًا مِنْهَا
إِنَّا إِلَىٰ رَبِّنَا رَاغِبُونَ ۝

33. Kad͟haalikal- 'Ad͟haab; wa la-'Ad͟haabul - Aak͟hirati 'akbar. Law kaanuu ya'-lamuun ! (Section 2)

٣٣- كَذَٰلِكَ الْعَذَابُ ۖ
وَلَعَذَابُ الْآخِرَةِ أَكْبَرُ ۚ
لَوْ كَانُوا يَعْلَمُونَ ۝

34. Inna lil-Muttaqiina 'inda Rabbihim Jannaatin-Na-'iim.

٣٤- إِنَّ لِلْمُتَّقِينَ عِنْدَ رَبِّهِمْ
جَنَّاتِ النَّعِيمِ ۝

30. Then they turned, one against another, in reproach.

31. They said: "Alas for us ! We have indeed transgressed !

32. " It may be that our Lord will give us in exchange A better (garden) than this: for we do turn to Him (in Repentance) "

33. Such is the Punishment (in this life); but greater is the Punishment In the Hereafter, if only they knew !

34. Verily, for the Righteous are gardens of Delight, In the Presence of their Lord.

35. 'Afanaj-'alul - Muslimiina kal-mujrimiin ?

٣٥- أَفَنَجْعَلُ الْمُسْلِمِينَ كَالْمُجْرِمِينَ ۝

36. Maa lakum ? kayfa tahku-muun ?

٣٦- مَا لَكُمْ كَيْفَ تَحْكُمُونَ ۝

37. Am lakum Kitaabun-fiihi tadrusuun -

٣٧- أَمْ لَكُمْ كِتٰبٌ فِيهِ تَدْرُسُونَ ۝

38. Inna lakum fiihi lamaa takhayyaruun ?

٣٨- إِنَّ لَكُمْ فِيهِ لَمَا تَخَيَّرُونَ ۝

39. Am lakum 'Aymaanun 'alaynaa baalighatun 'ilaa Yaw-mil - Qiyaamati 'inna lakum lamaa tah-kumuun ?

٣٩- أَمْ لَكُمْ أَيْمٰنٌ عَلَيْنَا
بٰلِغَةٌ إِلٰى يَوْمِ الْقِيٰمَةِ
إِنَّ لَكُمْ لَمَا تَحْكُمُونَ ۝

35. Shall We then treat the People of Faith Like the People of Sin ?

36. What is the matter with you ? How judge you ?

37. Or have you a Book through which you learn ?

38. That you shall have thtrough it whatever you choose ?

39. Or do you have covenants with Us on oath, Reaching to the Day of Judgement (providing) That you shall have whatever you shall demand ?

40. Sal-hum 'ayyuhum-bi-dhaa-
lika za-'iim !

۴۰- سَلْهُمْ اَيُّهُمْ بِذٰلِكَ زَعِيْمٌ ۚ

41. Am lahum shurakaaa-'u
fal-ya'-tuu bi-shurakaaa-'ihim
in-kaanuu saadiqiin !

۴۱- اَمْ لَهُمْ شُرَكَآءُ ۚ
فَلْيَاْتُوْا بِشُرَكَآئِهِمْ اِنْ كَانُوْا صٰدِقِيْنَ

42. Yawma yuk-shafu 'an-
saaqinw-wa yud-'awna 'ilas-
sujuudi falaa yasta-tii-'uun, ---

۴۲- يَوْمَ يُكْشَفُ عَنْ سَاقٍ
وَّيُدْعَوْنَ اِلَى السُّجُوْدِ
فَلَا يَسْتَطِيْعُوْنَ

43. Khaashi-'atan 'absaaruhum
tarhaquhum dhillah: wa qad
kaanuu yud-'awna 'ilas-sujuudi
wa hum saalimuun.

۴۳- خَاشِعَةً اَبْصَارُهُمْ تَرْهَقُهُمْ ذِلَّةٌ ۭ
وَقَدْ كَانُوْا يُدْعَوْنَ اِلَى السُّجُوْدِ
وَهُمْ سٰلِمُوْنَ

40. Ask you of them, which of them will stand, Surety for that !

41. Or have they some " partners " (in Godhead) ? Then let them produce their " partners, " If they are truthful !

42. The Day that the shin shall be laid bare, And they shall be summoned to bow In adoration, but they shall not be able,

43. Their eyes will be cast down, Ignominy will cover them; seeing that They had been summoned aforetime To bow in adoration, while they were whole, (And had refused).

44. Fadharnii wa many-yukadh-dhibu bi-haadhal-Hadiith: sanas-tadrijuhum-min haythu laa ya'-lamuun.	۴۴- فَذَرْنِي وَمَن يُكَذِّبُ بِهَٰذَا الْحَدِيثِ سَنَسْتَدْرِجُهُم مِّنْ حَيْثُ لَا يَعْلَمُونَ ○
45. Wa 'umlii lahum: 'inna kaydi matiin.	۴۵- وَأُمْلِي لَهُمْ إِنَّ كَيْدِي مَتِينٌ ○
46. Am tas-'aluhum 'ajran-fa-hum-mim - maghramim - muthqa-luun ?	۴۶- أَمْ تَسْأَلُهُمْ أَجْرًا فَهُم مِّن مَّغْرَمٍ مُّثْقَلُونَ ○
47. Am 'indahumul-Ghaybu fahum yaktubuun ?	۴۷- أَمْ عِندَهُمُ الْغَيْبُ فَهُمْ يَكْتُبُونَ ○
48. Fasbir li-Hukmi Rabbika wa laa takun-ka-Saahibil-Hut. Idh naadaa wa huwa mak-zuum.	۴۸- فَاصْبِرْ لِحُكْمِ رَبِّكَ وَلَا تَكُن كَصَاحِبِ الْحُوتِ إِذْ نَادَىٰ وَهُوَ مَكْظُومٌ ○

44. Then leave Me alone with such as reject This Message: by degrees shall We punish them From directionsthey perceive no

45. A (long) respite will I grant them: Truly Powerful is My Plan.

46. Or is it that you do ask them for a reward, So that they are burdened With a load of debt ?

47. Or that the Unseen is in their hands, So that they can write it down ?

49. Law laaa 'an-tadaarakahuu Ni'-matum-mir - Rabbihii lanu-bidha bil-'araaa-'i wa huwa madhmuum.

٤٩- لَوْلَآ اَنْ تَدٰرَكَهٗ
نِعْمَةٌ مِّنْ رَّبِّهٖ
لَنُبِذَ بِالْعَرَآءِ وَهُوَ مَذْمُوْمٌ ۝

50. Fa-jtabaahu Rabbuhuu fa-ja-'alahuu minas-Saalihiin.

٥٠- فَاجْتَبٰهُ رَبُّهٗ
فَجَعَلَهٗ مِنَ الصّٰلِحِيْنَ ۝

51. Wa iny - yakaadulladhiina kafaruu layuz-liquunaka bi-absaarihim lammaa sami-'udh-dhikra wa yaquuluuna 'innahuu la-majnuun !

٥١- وَاِنْ يَّكَادُ الَّذِيْنَ كَفَرُوْا لَيُزْلِقُوْنَكَ
بِاَبْصَارِهِمْ لَمَّا سَمِعُوا الذِّكْرَ
وَيَقُوْلُوْنَ اِنَّهٗ لَمَجْنُوْنٌ ۝

52. Wa maa huwa 'illaa dhikrul-lil-'Aalamiin. (Part One-Fourth)

٥٢- وَمَا هُوَ اِلَّا ذِكْرٌ لِّلْعٰلَمِيْنَ ۝

48. So wait with patience for the Command Of your Lord, and be notlLike the Companion Of the fish, when he cried out in agony.

49. Had not Grace from His Lord Reached him, he would indeed have been Cast off on the naked shore, in disgrace.

50. Thus did his Lord choose him and make him Of the company of the Righteous.

51. And the Unbelievers would almost Trip you up with their eyes when they say : " Surely he is possessed ! "

52. But it is nothing less than a Message To all the worlds.

سُورَةُ الحَآقَّةِ

Al Haqqah

جزء 29

Bismillaahir - Rahmaanir - Rahiim. بِسْمِ اللّٰهِ الرَّحْمٰنِ الرَّحِيْمِ

1. AL HAAAQQATU ! ١- اَلْحَآقَّةُ ۝

2. MAL-HAAAQQAH ? ٢- مَا الْحَآقَّةُ ۝

3. Wa maaa adraaka mal-Haaaqqah ? ٣- وَمَآ اَدْرٰىكَ مَا الْحَآقَّةُ ۝

4. Kadhdhabat Thamuudu wa 'Aa-dum-bil-Qaari-`ah ! ٤- كَذَّبَتْ ثَمُوْدُ وَعَادٌۢ بِالْقَارِعَةِ ۝

5. Fa-ammaa Thamuudu fa-uhlikuu bit-Taaghiyah ! ٥- فَاَمَّا ثَمُوْدُ فَاُهْلِكُوْا بِالطَّاغِيَةِ ۝

In the name of Allah, Most Gracious, Most Merciful.

1. The Sure Reality !

2. What is The Sure Reality !

3. And what will make you realize what The Sure Reality is ?

4. The Thamud and the `Ad peopl (Branded) as false the stunning Calamity !

5. But the Thamud, they were destroyed By a terrible Storm of thunder and lightening !

6. Wa ammaa `Aadun-fa-uh-likuu bi - Riihin - sarsarin `aatiyah;

٦- وَأَمَّا عَادٌ فَأُهْلِكُوا بِرِيحٍ صَرْصَرٍ عَاتِيَةٍ ۝

7. Sakh-kharahaa `alayhim sab-`a layaalinw-wa Thsamaa-niyata ayyaamin husuuman-fatara'l-qawma fiihaa sar-`aa ka-annahum a`-jaazu nakhlin khaawiyah !

٧- سَخَّرَهَا عَلَيْهِمْ سَبْعَ لَيَالٍ وَثَمَٰنِيَةَ أَيَّامٍ حُسُومًا فَتَرَى الْقَوْمَ فِيهَا صَرْعَىٰ كَأَنَّهُمْ أَعْجَازُ نَخْلٍ خَاوِيَةٍ ۝

8. Fahal taraa lahum-mim-baaqiyah ?

٨- فَهَلْ تَرَىٰ لَهُم مِّن بَاقِيَةٍ ۝

9. Wa jaaa-'a Fir-`awnu wa man-qablahuu wal-mu'-tafikaa-tu bil-khaati-'ah,

٩- وَجَاءَ فِرْعَوْنُ وَمَن قَبْلَهُ وَالْمُؤْتَفِكَاتُ بِالْخَاطِئَةِ ۝

6. And the `Ad, they were destroyed By a furious Wind, exceedingly violent;

7. He made it rage against them seven nights And eight days in succession: So that you could see the (whole) people lying Prostrate in its (path), as if they had been Roots of hollow palm-trees tumbled down !

8. Then do see you any of them left surviving ?

9. And Pharaoh, and those before him, And the Cities Overthrown. Committed habitual Sin,

10. Fa-`asaw rasuula Rabbihim fa akhadhahum akhdhatar-raa-biyah.

١٠- فَعَصَوْا رَسُولَ رَبِّهِمْ
فَأَخَذَهُمْ أَخْذَةً رَّابِيَةً ۝

11. Innaa lammaa taghal-maaa-'u hamalnaakum fil-jaa-riyah,

١١- إِنَّا لَمَّا طَغَا الْمَآءُ
حَمَلْنَٰكُمْ فِى الْجَارِيَةِ ۝

12. Linaj-`alahaa lakum Tadh-kiratanw-wa ta-`iyahaaa udhu-nunw-waa-`iyah.

١٢- لِنَجْعَلَهَا لَكُمْ تَذْكِرَةً
وَتَعِيَهَآ أُذُنٌ وَٰعِيَةٌ ۝

13. Fa-idhaa nufikha fis-Suuri naf-khatunw-waahidah,

١٣- فَإِذَا نُفِخَ فِى الصُّورِ نَفْخَةٌ وَٰحِدَةٌ ۝

14. Wa humilatil-ardu wal-jibaalu fadukkataa dakkatanw-waahidah, -

١٤- وَحُمِلَتِ الْأَرْضُ وَالْجِبَالُ
فَدُكَّتَا دَكَّةً وَٰحِدَةً ۝

10. And disobeyed (each) the Messenger Of their Lord; so He punished them With an abundant Penalty.

11. We, when the water (of Noah's Flood) Overflowed beyond its limits, Carried you (mankind), in the floating (Ark),

12. That We might make it a message Unto you, and that ears (that should hear the tale) And retain its memory should bear its (lessons) In rememberance.

13. Then, when one blast is sounded On the Trumpet,

14. And the earth is moved, and its mountains, And they are crushed to powder at one stroke,

١٥- فَيَوْمَئِذٍ وَقَعَتِ الْوَاقِعَةُ ۝

15. Fa - yawma - 'i<u>dh</u>inw-waqa-
`atil-Waaqi-`ah,

١٦- وَانشَقَّتِ السَّمَاءُ فَهِيَ يَوْمَئِذٍ وَاهِيَةٌ ۝

16. Wan-<u>sh</u>aqqatis-samaaa-'u
fahiya Yawma - 'i<u>dh</u>inw-waa-
hiyah,

١٧- وَالْمَلَكُ عَلَىٰ أَرْجَائِهَا ۚ
وَيَحْمِلُ عَرْشَ رَبِّكَ فَوْقَهُمْ
يَوْمَئِذٍ ثَمَانِيَةٌ ۝

17. Wal-malaku `alaaa 'arjaaa-
'ihaa, wa yahmilu `Ar<u>sh</u>a Rab-
bika fawqahum Yawma-'i<u>dh</u>in-
<u>th</u>amaaniyah.

١٨- يَوْمَئِذٍ تُعْرَضُونَ
لَا تَخْفَىٰ مِنكُمْ خَافِيَةٌ ۝

18. Yawma - 'i<u>dh</u>in-tu`-raduuna
laa ta<u>kh</u>faa minkum <u>kh</u>aafiyah.

١٩- فَأَمَّا مَنْ أُوتِيَ كِتَابَهُ بِيَمِينِهِ
فَيَقُولُ هَاؤُمُ اقْرَءُوا كِتَابِيَهْ ۝

19. Fa-ammaa man uutiya
Kitaabahuu bi-yamiinihii fa-
yaquulu haaa - 'u - muq-ra-'uu
Kitaabiyah !

15. On that Day shall the (Great) Event Come to pass,

16. And the sky will be Rent assunder, For it will that Day be flimsy,

17. And the angels will be on its sides, And eight will, that Day, bear the Throne Of your Lord above them.

18. That Day shall you be brought to Judgement: Not an act of yours that you hide Will be hidden.

19. Then he that will begiven his Record In his right hand will say: " Ah here ! Read you my Record !

20. Innii zanantu annii mulaaqin Hisaabiyah !

٢٠- إِنِّي ظَنَنتُ أَنِّي مُلَٰقٍ حِسَابِيَهْ ۝

21. Fa-huwa fii `iishatir-raadiyah,

٢١- فَهُوَ فِي عِيشَةٍ رَّاضِيَةٍ ۝

22. Fii Jannatin `aaliyah,

٢٢- فِي جَنَّةٍ عَالِيَةٍ ۝

23. Qutuufuhaa daaniyah.

٢٣- قُطُوفُهَا دَانِيَةٌ ۝

24. Kuluu wash-rabuu haniii-'am-bimaaa aslaftum fil-ayyaamil-khaaliyah

٢٤- كُلُوا وَاشْرَبُوا هَنِيٓـًٔا
بِمَآ أَسْلَفْتُمْ فِي الْأَيَّامِ الْخَالِيَةِ ۝

25. Wa ammaa man 'uutiya Kitaabahuu bi-shimaalihii fa-yaquulu yaa-laytanii lam 'uuta Kitaabiyah !

٢٥- وَأَمَّا مَنْ أُوتِيَ كِتَٰبَهُۥ بِشِمَالِهِۦ
فَيَقُولُ يَٰلَيْتَنِي
لَمْ أُوتَ كِتَٰبِيَهْ ۝

20. " I did really understand that My account would (One Day) reach me ! "

21. And he will be in a life of Bliss,

22. In a Garden on high,

23. The Fruits whereof (Will hang in bunches) low and near.

24. " Eat you and drink you, with Full satisfaction; because of the (good) That you sent before you, In the days that are gone ! "

25. And he that will be given his Record In his left hand, will say: " Ah ! would That my record had not been given to me! "

26. Wa lam adri maa hisaa-biyah !

٢٦-وَلَمْ أَدْرِ مَا حِسَابِيَهْ ۝

27. Yaa-laytahaa kaanatil-qaadiyah !

٢٧-يٰلَيْتَهَا كَانَتِ الْقَاضِيَةَ ۝

28. Maaa aghnaa `annii maa-liyah !

٢٨-مَآ أَغْنٰى عَنِّى مَالِيَهْ ۝

29. Halaka `annii sul-taaniyah !

٢٩-هَلَكَ عَنِّى سُلْطٰنِيَهْ ۝

30. Khudhuuhu faghulluh,

٣٠-خُذُوهُ فَغُلُّوهُ ۝

31. Thummal-Jahiima salluuh,

٣١-ثُمَّ الْجَحِيمَ صَلُّوهُ ۝

26. " And that I had never realized how My account (stood) !

27. " Ah ! would that (Death) Had made an end of me !

28. " Of no profit to me has been my wealth !

29. " My power has perished from me !

30. The stern command will say: " Seize you him, and bind yoy him,

31. " And burn you him in the Blazing Fire,

32. Thumma fii sil-silatin-dhar-`uhaa sab-`uuna dhiraa-`an-fasluкuuh !

٣٢- ثُمَّ فِي سِلْسِلَةٍ ذَرْعُهَا سَبْعُونَ ذِرَاعًا فَاسْلُكُوهُ ۝

33. Innahuu kaana laa yu'-minu billaahil-`Aziimi,

٣٣- إِنَّهُ كَانَ لَا يُؤْمِنُ بِاللَّهِ الْعَظِيمِ ۝

34. Wa laa yahuzzu `alaa ta-`aamil-miskiin !

٣٤- وَلَا يَحُضُّ عَلَىٰ طَعَامِ الْمِسْكِينِ ۝

35. Falaysa lahul-Yawma haa-hunaa hamiim,

٣٥- فَلَيْسَ لَهُ الْيَوْمَ هَاهُنَا حَمِيمٌ ۝

36. Wa laa ta-`aamun 'illaa min ghisliin,

٣٦- وَلَا طَعَامٌ إِلَّا مِنْ غِسْلِينٍ ۝

37. Laa ya'-kuluhuuu 'illal-khaati-'uun.

٣٧- لَا يَأْكُلُهُ إِلَّا الْخَاطِئُونَ ۝

32. " Further, make him march in a chain, Whereof the length is seventy cubits !

33. " This was he that would not believe In Allah Most High,

34. " And would not encourage The feeding of the indigent !

35. " So no friend Has he here this Day,

36. " Nor Has he any food except the corruption From the washing of wounds,

37. " Which none do eat but those in sin. "

38. Falaaa 'uqsimu bimaa tub-siruun

۳۸-فَلَآ اُقۡسِمُ بِمَا تُبۡصِرُوۡنَ ۙ

39. Wa maa laa tubsiruun,

۳۹-وَمَا لَا تُبۡصِرُوۡنَ ۙ

40. Innahuu la-qawlu Rasuu-lin-Kariim;

۴۰-اِنَّهٗ لَقَوۡلُ رَسُوۡلٍ كَرِيۡمٍ ۚ

41. Wa maa huwa bi-qawli shaa-`ir: qaliilam-maa tu'-mi-nuun !

۴۱-وَّمَا هُوَ بِقَوۡلِ شَاعِرٍ ؕ
قَلِيۡلًا مَّا تُؤۡمِنُوۡنَ ۙ

42. Wa laa bi-qawli-kaahin: qaliilam-maa tadhakkaruun.

۴۲-وَلَا بِقَوۡلِ كَاهِنٍ ؕ
قَلِيۡلًا مَّا تَذَكَّرُوۡنَ ؕ

43. Tanziilum-mir-Rabbil-`Aa lamiin,

۴۳-تَنۡزِيۡلٌ مِّنۡ رَّبِّ الۡعٰلَمِيۡنَ ○

38. So I do call to witness What you see

39. And what you donot see,

40. That this is verily the world Of an honored Messenger;

41. It is not the word of a Poet: Little it is you believe !

42. Nor is it the word of a soothsayer: Little admonition it is you receive.

43. (This is) a Message sent down from the Lord of the worlds.

44. Wa law taqawwala `alaynaa ba`-da'l-'aqaawiil,

٤٤- وَلَوْ تَقَوَّلَ عَلَيْنَا بَعْضَ الْأَقَاوِيلِ ○

45. La-akhadhnaa minhu bil-yamiin,

٤٥- لَأَخَذْنَا مِنْهُ بِالْيَمِينِ ○

46. Thumma laqata`-naa minhul-watiin:

٤٦- ثُمَّ لَقَطَعْنَا مِنْهُ الْوَتِينَ ○

47. Famaa minkum - min ahadin `anhu haajiziin.

٤٧- فَمَا مِنكُم مِّنْ أَحَدٍ عَنْهُ حَاجِزِينَ ○

48. Wa innahuu la-Tadhkiratul-lil-Muttaqiin.

٤٨- وَإِنَّهُ لَتَذْكِرَةٌ لِّلْمُتَّقِينَ ○

44. And if the Messenger were to invent Any sayings in Our name,

45. We should certainly seize him By his right hand,

46. And We should certainly Then cut off the artery of his heart:

47. Nor could any of you withhold him (From Our wrath)

48. But verily this is a Message for The God-fearing.

49. Wa innaa lana`-lamu anna minkum-mukadh-dhibiin.

٤٩-وَاِنَّا لَنَعْلَمُ اَنَّ مِنْكُمْ مُّكَذِّبِيْنَ ○

50. Wa innahuu la-hasratun `alal-kaafiriin.

٥٠-وَاِنَّهٗ لَحَسْرَةٌ عَلَى الْكٰفِرِيْنَ ○

51. Wa innahuu la-Haqqul-yaqiin.

٥١-وَاِنَّهٗ لَحَقُّ الْيَقِيْنِ ○

52. Fasabbih bismi Rabbikal-`Aziim.

٥٢-فَسَبِّحْ بِاسْمِ رَبِّكَ الْعَظِيْمِ ○

49. And We certainly know that there are Amongst you those that reject (it).

50. But truly (Revelation) in a cause of sorrow For the Unbelievers.

51. But verily it is Truth of assured certainty.

52. So glorify the name of your Lord Most High.

سُورَةُ المعَارِج

Al Ma'arij

جزء 29

Bismillahir - Rahmaanir - Rahiim. بِسْمِ اللّٰهِ الرَّحْمٰنِ الرَّحِيْمِ

1. Sa-'ala saaa-'ilum-bi-`Adhaa-binw-waaqi`,

١- سَاَلَ سَآئِلٌۢ بِعَذَابٍ وَّاقِعٍ ۙ

2. Lil-kaafiriina laysa lahuu daafi`,

٢- لِّلْكٰفِرِيْنَ لَيْسَ لَهٗ دَافِعٌ ۙ

3. Mina-llaahi DHil-MA-`AARIJ.

٣- مِّنَ اللّٰهِ ذِى الْمَعَارِجِ ؕ

4. Ta`-rujul-malaaa-'ikatu war-Ruuhu ilayhi fii Yawmin-kaa-na miq-daaruhuu khamsiina alfa sanah:

٤- تَعْرُجُ الْمَلٰٓئِكَةُ وَالرُّوْحُ اِلَيْهِ فِىْ يَوْمٍ كَانَ مِقْدَارُهٗ خَمْسِيْنَ اَلْفَ سَنَةٍ ۚ

5. Fasbir Sabran-jamililaa.

٥- فَاصْبِرْ صَبْرًا جَمِيْلًا

In the name of Allah, Most Gracious, Most Merciful.

1. A questioner asked About a Penalty to befall

2. The Unbeliever the which there is none To ward off,

3. (A Penalty) from Allah, Lord of the Ways of Ascent.

4. The angels and the Spirit ascend Unto Him in a Day the measure whereof Is (as) fifty yousand years:

5. Therefore do you hold patience, A patience of beautiful (contentment).

٦-إِنَّهُمْ يَرَوْنَهُ بَعِيدًا ۙ

6. Innahum yarawnahuu ba-`iidaa:

٧-وَنَرَاهُ قَرِيبًا ۚ

7. Wa naraahu qariibaa.

٨-يَوْمَ تَكُونُ السَّمَاءُ كَالْمُهْلِ ۙ

8. Yawma takuunus-samaaa-'u kal-muhl,

٩-وَتَكُونُ الْجِبَالُ كَالْعِهْنِ ۙ

9. Wa takuunul - jibaalu kal-`ihn,

١٠-وَلَا يَسْأَلُ حَمِيمٌ حَمِيمًا ۚ

10. Wa laa yas-'alu hamiimun hamiimaa,

١١-يُبَصَّرُونَهُمْ ۚ
يَوَدُّ الْمُجْرِمُ لَوْ
يَفْتَدِي مِنْ عَذَابِ يَوْمِئِذٍ بِبَنِيهِ ۙ

11. Yubassaruunahum,: ya-waddul-mujrimu law yaftadii min `Adhaabi Yaw-mi-'idhim-bi-baniih,

6. They see the (Day) indeed As a far-off (event):

7. But We see it (quite) near.

8. The Day that Tte sky will be like Molten brass,

9. And the mountains will be like wool,

10. And no friend will ask after a friend,

11. though they will be put In sight of each other, The sinner's desire will be: Would that he could redeem himself from the Penalty of that Day By (sacrificing) his children,

12. Wa saahibatihii wa akhiih,
١٢- وَصَاحِبَتِهٖ وَاَخِيْهِ ۝

13. Wa fasiilatihi-llatii tu'-wiih,
١٣- وَفَصِيْلَتِهِ الَّتِىْ تُـْٔوِيْهِ ۝

14. Wa man fil-ardi jamii-`an- Thumma yunjiih;
١٤- وَمَنْ فِى الْاَرْضِ جَمِيْعًا ۙ ثُمَّ يُنْجِيْهِ ۝

15. Kallaa ! innahaa lazaa !
١٥- كَلَّا ۭ اِنَّهَا لَظٰى ۝

16. Nazzaa-`atal-lish-shawaa !
١٦- نَزَّاعَةً لِّلشَّوٰى ۝

17. Tad-`uu man adbara wa tawallaa,
١٧- تَدْعُوْا مَنْ اَدْبَرَ وَتَوَلّٰى ۝

18. Wa jama-`a fa-aw-`aa !
١٨- وَجَمَعَ فَاَوْعٰى ۝

12. His wife and his brother,

13. His kindred who sheltered him,

14. And all, that is on earth, So it could deliver him:

15. By no means ! for it would be The Fire of Hell !

16. Plucking out (his being) Right to the skull !

17. Inviting (all) such as turn their backs And turn away their faces (From the Right),

18. And collect (wealth) and hide it (from use) !

19. Innal - insaana khuliqa haluu-`aa;

١٩- إِنَّ الْإِنسَانَ خُلِقَ هَلُوعًا ۝

20. Idhaa massahush-sharru jazuu-`aa;

٢٠- إِذَا مَسَّهُ الشَّرُّ جَزُوعًا ۝

21. Wa idhaa massahul-khayru manuu-`aa;

٢١- وَإِذَا مَسَّهُ الْخَيْرُ مَنُوعًا ۝

22. Illal-Musalliin;

٢٢- إِلَّا الْمُصَلِّينَ ۝

23. Alladhiina hum `alaa Salaati-him daaa-'imuun;

٢٣- الَّذِينَ هُمْ عَلَىٰ صَلَاتِهِمْ دَائِمُونَ ۝

24. Walladhiina fiii amwaali-him haqqum-ma`-luum

٢٤- وَالَّذِينَ فِي أَمْوَالِهِمْ حَقٌّ مَّعْلُومٌ ۝

25. Lis-saaa-'ili wal - mah-ruum;

٢٥- لِّلسَّائِلِ وَالْمَحْرُومِ ۝

19. Truly man was created very impatient;

20. Fretful when evil touches him;

21. And niggardly when good reaches him;

22. Not so those devoted to Prayer,

23. Those who remain steadfast to their prayer;

24. And those in whose wealth Is a recognized right

25. For the (needy) who asks And him who is prevented (For some reason from asking):

26. Walla<u>dh</u>iina yusaddiquuna bi-Yawmid-Diin;

٢٦- وَالَّذِينَ يُصَدِّقُونَ بِيَوْمِ الدِّينِ ۝

27. Walla<u>dh</u>iina-hum-min `a<u>dh</u>aa-bi Rabbihim mu<u>sh</u>fiquun,

٢٧- وَالَّذِينَ هُم مِّنْ عَذَابِ رَبِّهِم مُّشْفِقُونَ ۝

28. Inna `a<u>dh</u>aaba Rabbihim <u>gh</u>ayru ma' -muun;

٢٨- إِنَّ عَذَابَ رَبِّهِمْ غَيْرُ مَأْمُونٍ ۝

29. Walla<u>dh</u>iina hum li-furuuji-him haafizuun,

٢٩- وَالَّذِينَ هُمْ لِفُرُوجِهِمْ حَافِظُونَ ۝

30. Illaa `alaaa azwaajihim aw maa malakat aymaanuhum fa-innahum <u>gh</u>ayru maluumiin,

٣٠- إِلَّا عَلَىٰ أَزْوَاجِهِمْ أَوْ مَا مَلَكَتْ أَيْمَانُهُمْ
فَإِنَّهُمْ غَيْرُ مَلُومِينَ ۝

31. Famani-ibta<u>gh</u>aa waraaa-'a <u>dh</u>aalika fa-'ulaaa-'ika humul-`aaduun ;

٣١- فَمَنِ ابْتَغَىٰ وَرَاءَ ذَٰلِكَ فَأُولَٰئِكَ هُمُ الْعَادُونَ ۝

26. And those who hold To the truth of the Day of Judgement;

27. And those who fear The displeasure of their Lord,

28. For their Lord's displeasure Is the opposite of Peace and Tranquility;

29. And those who guard their chastity,

30. Except with their wives and those whom Their right hand possess, For (then) they are not to be blamed,

31. But those who trespass Beyond this are transgressors;

32. Walladhiina hum li-amaa-naatihim wa `ahdihim raa-`uun ;

٣٢-وَالَّذِيْنَ هُمْ لِاَمٰنٰتِهِمْ وَعَهْدِهِمْ رٰعُوْنَ ۝

33. Walladhiina hum-bi-shahaa-daatihim qaaa-'imuun;

٣٣-وَالَّذِيْنَ هُمْ بِشَهٰدٰتِهِمْ قَآئِمُوْنَ ۝

34. Walladhiina hum `alaa Salaa-tihim yuhaafizuun;

٣٤-وَالَّذِيْنَ هُمْ عَلٰى صَلَاتِهِمْ يُحَافِظُوْنَ ۝

35. Ulaaa-'ika fii Jannaatim-mukramuun.

٣٥-اُولٰٓئِكَ فِيْ جَنّٰتٍ مُّكْرَمُوْنَ ۝

36. Famaa-lilladhiina kafaruu qibalaka muhti-`iin

٣٦-فَمَالِ الَّذِيْنَ كَفَرُوْا
قِبَلَكَ مُهْطِعِيْنَ ۝

32. And those who respect Their trust and covenants:

33. And those who stand firm In their testimonies;

34. And those who guard
(The sacredness) of their worship;

35. Such will be the honored ones In the garden of (Bliss).

36. Now what is the matter with the UnbelieversThat they rush madly before you -

37. `Anil-yamiini wa `anish-
shimaali `iziin ?

٣٧- عَنِ الْيَمِيْنِ وَعَنِ الشِّمَالِ عِزِيْنَ ○

38. A-yatma-`u kullum-ri-'im-
minhum any-yud-khala Jan-
nata Na-`iim ?

٣٨- اَيَطْمَعُ كُلُّ امْرِئٍ مِّنْهُمْ
اَنْ يُّدْخَلَ جَنَّةَ نَعِيْمٍ ○

39. Kallaa ! Innaa khalaqnaa-
hum-mimmaa ya`-lamuun !

٣٩- كَلَّا ۭ اِنَّا خَلَقْنٰهُمْ مِّمَّا يَعْلَمُوْنَ ○

40. Falaa uqsimu bi-Rab-
bil-Mashaariqi wal-Maghaaribi
innaa la-Qaadiruun

٤٠- فَلَآ اُقْسِمُ
بِرَبِّ الْمَشٰرِقِ وَالْمَغٰرِبِ اِنَّا لَقٰدِرُوْنَ ○

37. From the right and from the left iIn crowds ?

38. Does every man of them long to enter The Garden of Bliss ?

39. By no means ! For we have created them Out of the (base matter) they know !

40. Now I do call to witness The Lord of all points in the East And the West that We can certainly

41. `Alaaa an-nubaddila khay-ram-minhum wa maa Nahnu bi-masbuuqiin.

٤١- عَلَىٰٓ أَن نُّبَدِّلَ خَيْرًا مِّنْهُمْ
وَمَا نَحْنُ بِمَسْبُوقِينَ ۝

42. Fadharhum yakhuuduu wa yal-`abuu hattaa yulaaquu Yaw-mahumulladhi yuu-`aduun !

٤٢- فَذَرْهُمْ يَخُوضُوا وَيَلْعَبُوا
حَتَّىٰ يُلَٰقُوا
يَوْمَهُمُ الَّذِي يُوعَدُونَ ۝

43. Yawma yakhrujuuna minal - ajdaathi siraa-`an-ka-annahum ilaa nusubiny-yuufiduun,

٤٣- يَوْمَ يَخْرُجُونَ
مِنَ الْأَجْدَاثِ سِرَاعًا
كَأَنَّهُمْ إِلَىٰ نُصُبٍ يُوفِضُونَ ۝

44. Khaashi-`atan absaaruhum tarhaquhum dhillah ! Dhaalikal-Yawmulladhii kaanuu yuu-`aduun !

٤٤- خَاشِعَةً أَبْصَارُهُمْ
تَرْهَقُهُمْ ذِلَّةٌ ذَٰلِكَ الْيَوْمُ الَّذِي
كَانُوا يُوعَدُونَ ۝

41. Substitute for them better (men) than they; And we are not to be defeated (in Our Plan).

42. So leave them to plunge in vain talk And play about until they encounter That Day of theirs which They have been promised ! -

43. The Day whereon they will issue From their sepulchres in sudden haste Aṣ if they were bshing to a goal-post (Fixed for them),

44. Their eyes lowered in dejection, Ignominy covering them (all over) ! Such is the Day the which they Are promised !

سُورَةُ نُوح

Al Nūh

جزء 29

بِسْمِ ٱللَّهِ ٱلرَّحْمَٰنِ ٱلرَّحِيمِ

Bismillaahir - Rahmaanir - Rahiim.

١-إِنَّآ أَرْسَلْنَا نُوحًا إِلَىٰ قَوْمِهِۦٓ
أَنْ أَنذِرْ قَوْمَكَ مِن قَبْلِ
أَن يَأْتِيَهُمْ عَذَابٌ أَلِيمٌ ○

1. Innaaa arsalnaa NUUHAN ilaa Qawmihiii an andhir Qawmaka min-qabli any-ya-'tiyahum `Adhaabun aliim.

٢-قَالَ يَٰقَوْمِ
إِنِّى لَكُمْ نَذِيرٌ مُّبِينٌ ○

2. Qaala yaa-Qawmi innii lakum Nadhiirum-mubiin:

٣-أَنِ ٱعْبُدُوا۟ ٱللَّهَ
وَٱتَّقُوهُ وَأَطِيعُونِ ○

3. Ani-`budullaaha wattaquuhu wa atii-`uun:

In the name of Allah, Most Gracious, Most Merciful.

1. We sent Noah to his People (with the Command): " Do you warn your People Before there comes to them a grievous Penalty. "

2. He said: " O my People ! I am to you A Warner, clear and open:

3. That yoy should worship Allah, Fear Him, and obey me:

4. Yaghfir lakum-min-dhunuubi-kum wa yu-akh-khirkum ilaaa Ajalim - Musammaa: inna Ajallaahi 'idhaa jaaa-'a laa yu - 'akh-khar. Law kuntum ta`-lamuun.

٤-يَغْفِرْ لَكُمْ مِّنْ ذُنُوْبِكُمْ
وَيُؤَخِّرْكُمْ إِلَىٰٓ أَجَلٍ مُّسَمًّى
إِنَّ أَجَلَ اللّٰهِ إِذَا جَآءَ لَا يُؤَخَّرُ
لَوْ كُنْتُمْ تَعْلَمُوْنَ ○

5. Qaala Rabbi innii da-`awtu Qawmii lay-lanw-wa nahaaraa:

٥-قَالَ رَبِّ
إِنِّيْ دَعَوْتُ قَوْمِيْ لَيْلًا وَّنَهَارًا ○

6. Falam yazid-hum du-`aaa-iii illaa firaaraa.

٦-فَلَمْ يَزِدْهُمْ دُعَآءِيْٓ إِلَّا فِرَارًا ○

4. " So He may forgive you your sins And give you respite for a stated Term: For when the Term given by Allah Is accomplished, it cannot be put forward If you only knew. "

5. He said: " O my Lord ! I have called to My People Night and Day:

6. " But my call only increases (their) flight (From the Right).

7. Wa innii kullamaa da-awtu-hum li-taghfira lahum ja-`aluuu asaabi-`ahum fiii aadhaanihim was-tagh-shaw thiyaabahum wa asarruu was-tak-barus-tikbaa-raa.

٧- وَإِنِّي كُلَّمَا دَعَوْتُهُمْ لِتَغْفِرَ لَهُمْ جَعَلُوٓا أَصَابِعَهُمْ فِيٓ ءَاذَانِهِمْ وَاسْتَغْشَوْا ثِيَابَهُمْ وَأَصَرُّوا وَاسْتَكْبَرُوا اسْتِكْبَارًا ۝

8. Thumma innii da-`awtuhum jihaaraa;

٨- ثُمَّ إِنِّي دَعَوْتُهُمْ جِهَارًا ۝

9. Thumma inniii a`-lantu lahum wa asrartu lahum israa-raa,

٩- ثُمَّ إِنِّيٓ أَعْلَنتُ لَهُمْ وَأَسْرَرْتُ لَهُمْ إِسْرَارًا ۝

10. Faqult-us-taghfiruu Rab-bakum; innahuu kaana Ghaf-faaraa;

١٠- فَقُلْتُ اسْتَغْفِرُوا رَبَّكُمْ إِنَّهُۥ كَانَ غَفَّارًا ۝

7. " And every time I have Called to them, that You might forgive them, They have (only) thrust Their fingers into their ears Covered themselves up with Their garments, grown obstinate, And given themselves up to arrogance.

8. " So I have called to them aloud;

9. " Further I have spoken to them in public And secretly in private,

10. " Saying, 'Ask forgiveness from your Lord; For He is Oft-Forgiving;

11. Yursilis-samaaa-a `alay-
kum-midraaraa;

١١- يُرْسِلِ السَّمَآءَ عَلَيْكُمْ مِّدْرَارًا ۙ

12. Wa yumdidkum-bi-amwaa-
linw-wa baniina wa yaj-`al-la-
kum Jannaatinw-wa yaj-`al-
lakum anhaaraa.

١٢- وَّيُمْدِدْكُمْ بِأَمْوَالٍ وَّبَنِيْنَ وَيَجْعَلْ لَّكُمْ
جَنّٰتٍ وَّيَجْعَلْ لَّكُمْ أَنْهٰرًا ۗ

13. Maa lakum laa tarjuuna
lillaahi waqaaraa,

١٣- مَا لَكُمْ
لَا تَرْجُوْنَ لِلّٰهِ وَقَارًا ۚ

14. Wa qalakhalaqakum
atwaaraa ?

١٤- وَقَدْ خَلَقَكُمْ أَطْوَارًا

15. Alam taraw kayfa kha-
laqallaahu sab-`a samaawaatin
tibaaqa,

١٥- أَلَمْ تَرَوْا كَيْفَ خَلَقَ اللّٰهُ
سَبْعَ سَمٰوٰتٍ طِبَاقًا ۙ

11. " He will send rain to you in abundance;

12. " 'Give you increasein wealth and sons; And bestow on you gardens and Bestow on you rivers (of flowing water).

13. " 'What is the matter with you, that you Place not your hope For kindness and long-suffering in Allah,

14. " 'Seeing that it is He that has created you In diverse stages ?

15. " 'See you not how Allah has created The seven heavens one above another,

16. Wa ja-`alal-qamara fiihinna nuuranw-wa ja-`ala<u>sh</u>-<u>sh</u>amsa Siraajaa ?

١٦- وَّجَعَلَ الْقَمَرَ فِيْهِنَّ نُوْرًا
وَّجَعَلَ الشَّمْسَ سِرَاجًا ○

17. Wallaahu ambatakum-mi-nal-ardi nabaataa,

١٧- وَاللّٰهُ اَنْۢبَتَكُمْ
مِّنَ الْاَرْضِ نَبَاتًا ○

18. <u>Th</u>umma yu-`iidukum fiihaa wa yu<u>kh</u>rijukum i<u>kh</u>raajaa.

١٨- ثُمَّ يُعِيْدُكُمْ فِيْهَا
وَيُخْرِجُكُمْ اِخْرَاجًا ○

19. Wallaahu ja-`ala lakumul-arda bisaataa,

١٩- وَاللّٰهُ جَعَلَ لَكُمُ الْاَرْضَ بِسَاطًا ○

20. Litaslukuu minhaa subulan-fijaajaa.

٢٠- لِّتَسْلُكُوْا مِنْهَا سُبُلًا فِجَاجًا ○

16. " 'And madethe moon a light in their midst, And made the sun as a (glorious) Lamp ?

17. " 'And Allah has produced You from the earth, growing (gradually)

18. " 'And in the End He will return you Into the (earth), and raise you forth (Again at the Resurrection) ?

19. " 'And Allah has made the earth for you As a carpet (spread out),

20. " 'That you may go about Therein, in spacious roads.

21. Qaala Nuuhur - Rabbi in-
nahum `asawnii wattaba-`uu
mallam yazidhu maaluhu wa
waladuhuu illaa khassaraa.

٢١-قَالَ نُوحٌ رَّبِّ إِنَّهُمْ عَصَوْنِي
وَاتَّبَعُوا مَن لَّمْ يَزِدْهُ مَالُهُ وَوَلَدُهُ
إِلَّا خَسَارًا ۝

22. Wa makaruu Makran
kubbaaraa.

٢٢-وَمَكَرُوا مَكْرًا كُبَّارًا ۝

23. Wa qaaluu laa tadharunna
aalihatakum wa laa tadharunna
Waddanw-wa laa Suwaa-`aa, wa
laa Yaghuutha wa Ya-`uuqa wa
Nasraa;

٢٣-وَقَالُوا لَا تَذَرُنَّ آلِهَتَكُمْ
وَلَا تَذَرُنَّ وَدًّا وَلَا سُوَاعًا ۥ
وَلَا يَغُوثَ وَيَعُوقَ وَنَسْرًا ۝

24. Wa qad azalluu kathiiraa;
wa laa tazidiz-zaalimiina illaa
dalaalaa.

٢٤-وَقَدْ أَضَلُّوا كَثِيرًا ۥ
وَلَا تَزِدِ
الظَّالِمِينَ إِلَّا ضَلَالًا ۝

21. Noah said: " O my Lord ! They have disobeyed me, But they follow men) Whose wealth and children
Give them no Increase but only Loss.

22. " And they have devised a tremendous Plot.

23. " And they have said (to each other), 'Abandon not your gods; abandon Neither Wadd nor Suwa`, neither
Yaghuth nor Ya`uq, nor Nasr;

24. " They have already misled many; and Grant you no increase To the wrong-doers but in Straying (from their mark). "

25. Mimmaa khatiii-'aatihim ughriquu fa-ud-khiluu Naaraa: falam yajiduu lahum-min-duu-nillaahi ansaaraa.

۲۵- مِمَّا خَطِيْٓـٰتِهِمْ اُغْرِقُوْا
فَاُدْخِلُوْا نَارًا ۵
فَلَمْ يَجِدُوْا لَهُمْ
مِّنْ دُوْنِ اللّٰهِ اَنْصَارًا ○

26. Wa qaala Nuuhur - Rabbi laa tadhar `alal-ardi minal-kaa-firiina dayyaaraa !

۲۶- وَقَالَ نُوْحٌ رَّبِّ لَا تَذَرْ
عَلَى الْاَرْضِ مِنَ الْكٰفِرِيْنَ دَيَّارًا ○

27. Innaka in-tadharhum yu-dilluu `ibaadaka wa laa ya-liduuu illaa faajiran-kaffaaraa.

۲۷- اِنَّكَ اِنْ تَذَرْهُمْ
يُضِلُّوْا عِبَادَكَ
وَلَا يَلِدُوْٓا اِلَّا فَاجِرًا كَفَّارًا ○

28. Rabbi-igh-fir lii wa liwaali-dayya wa liman-dakhala bay-tiya Mu'-minanwa-wa lil-Mu'-miniina wal-Mu'-minaat: wa laa tazidiz-zaalimiina illaa tabaaraa !

۲۸- رَبِّ اغْفِرْ لِيْ وَلِوَالِدَيَّ
وَلِمَنْ دَخَلَ بَيْتِيَ مُؤْمِنًا
وَّلِلْمُؤْمِنِيْنَ وَالْمُؤْمِنٰتِ ؕ
وَلَا تَزِدِ الظّٰلِمِيْنَ اِلَّا تَبَارًا ○ ع

25. Because of their sins they were drowned (In the flood), and were made to enter The Fire (of Punishment): And they found in lieu of Allah None to help them.

26. And Noah said: " O my Lord ! Leave not Of the Unbelievers, a single one on earth !

27. " For, if You do leave (any of) them, They will but mislead Your devotees, And they will breed none But wicked ungrateful ones.

28. " O my Lord ! Forgive me, my parents, All who enter my house in Faith, And (all) believing men and believing women: And to the wrong-doers grant You no increase But in Perdition !

سُورَةُ الجِنّ

Al Jinn

جزء 29

Bismillaahir - Rahmaanir - Rahiim. بِسْمِ اللّٰهِ الرَّحْمٰنِ الرَّحِيْمِ

1. Qul uuhiya ilayya anna-
hu-stama-'a nafarum - minal-
JINNI faqaaluuu innaa sami`-
naa Qur-'aanan `ajabaa,

١- قُلْ أُوْحِيَ إِلَيَّ
أَنَّهُ اسْتَمَعَ نَفَرٌ مِّنَ الْجِنِّ
فَقَالُوْا إِنَّا سَمِعْنَا قُرْاٰنًا عَجَبًا ۙ

2. Yahdii ilar-Rushdi fa-'aa-
mannaa bih: wa lan-nushrika
bi-Rabbinaaa ahadaa.

٢- يَّهْدِيْ إِلَى الرُّشْدِ
فَاٰمَنَّا بِهٖ ؕ
وَلَنْ نُّشْرِكَ بِرَبِّنَآ أَحَدًا ۙ

3. Wa annahuu Ta-`aalaa Jad-
du Rabbinaa m'attakhadha saa-
hibatanw-wa laa waladaa.

٣- وَّأَنَّهٗ تَعٰلٰى جَدُّ رَبِّنَا
مَا اتَّخَذَ صَاحِبَةً وَّلَا وَلَدًا ۙ

4. Wa annahuu kaana yaquulu
safiihunaa `ala-Allaahi shatataa;

٤- وَّأَنَّهٗ كَانَ يَقُوْلُ سَفِيْهُنَا
عَلَى اللّٰهِ شَطَطًا ۙ

In the name of Allah, Most Gracious, Most Merciful.

1. Say: It has been revealed to me that A company of Jinns listened (to the Qur'an) They said, 'We have really heard A wonderful recital !

2. It gives guidance to the Right And we have believed therein: We shall not join (in worship) Any (gods) with our Lord.

3. And exalted is the Majesty Of our Lord: He has taken neither A wife nor a son.

4. 'There were some foolish ones Among us, who used to utter Extravagant lies against Allah;

5. Wa annaa zanannaaa allan-
taquulal-insu wal-jinnu `ala
Allaahi kadhibaa.

٥-وَّاَنَّا ظَنَنَّآ اَنْ لَّنْ تَقُوْلَ الْاِنْسُ وَالْجِنُّ
عَلَى اللّٰهِ كَذِبًا ۙ

6. Wa annahuu kaana rijaa-
lum-minal-insi ya-`uudhuuna bi-
rijaalim-minal-Jinni fazaaduu-
hum rahaqaa.

٦-وَّاَنَّهٗ كَانَ رِجَالٌ مِّنَ الْاِنْسِ
يَعُوْذُوْنَ بِرِجَالٍ مِّنَ الْجِنِّ
فَزَادُوْهُمْ رَهَقًا ۙ

7. Wa annahum zannuu kamaa
zanantum allany-yab-`atha
Allaahu ahadaa.

٧-وَّاَنَّهُمْ ظَنُّوْا كَمَا ظَنَنْتُمْ
اَنْ لَّنْ يَّبْعَثَ اللّٰهُ اَحَدًا ۙ

8. Wa annaa lamasnas-
samaaa-'a fawajadnaahaa mu-
li-'at harasan-shadiidanw-wa
shuhubaa.

٨-وَّاَنَّا لَمَسْنَا السَّمَآءَ
فَوَجَدْنٰهَا مُلِئَتْ حَرَسًا
شَدِيْدًا وَّشُهُبًا ۙ

5. But we do think that no man Or spirit should say aught that is Untrue against Allah.

6. True, there were persons Among mankind who took shelter With persons among the Jinns, But they increased them in folly.

7. And they (came to) think As you thought, that Allah would not Raise up anyone (to Judgement).

8. And we pried into the secrets of heaven; But we found it filled with stern guards And flaming fires.

9. Wa annaa kunnaa naq-`udu minhaa maqaa-'ida lis-sam`i ; famany-yastami-'il-'aana yajid lahuu shihaabar-rasadaa.

٩- وَأَنَّا كُنَّا نَقْعُدُ مِنْهَا مَقَاعِدَ لِلسَّمْعِ
فَمَنْ يَسْتَمِعِ الْآنَ يَجِدْ لَهُ
شِهَابًا رَّصَدًا ۝

10. Wa annaa laa nadriii a-sharrun uriida biman-fil-ardi am araada bihim Rabbuhum rashadaa.

١٠- وَأَنَّا لَا نَدْرِي أَشَرٌّ
أُرِيدَ بِمَنْ فِي الْأَرْضِ
أَمْ أَرَادَ بِهِمْ رَبُّهُمْ رَشَدًا ۝

11. Wa annaa minnas-saali-huuna wa minnaa duuna dhaalik: kunnaa taraaa-'iqa qidadaa.

١١- وَأَنَّا مِنَّا الصَّلِحُونَ وَمِنَّا دُونَ
ذَٰلِكَ كُنَّا طَرَآئِقَ قِدَدًا ۝

12. Wa annaa zanannaaa allan-nu`-jiza-Allaaha fil-ardi wa lan-nu`-jizahu harabaa.

١٢- وَأَنَّا ظَنَنَّآ أَنْ لَّنْ نُّعْجِزَ اللّٰهَ فِي
الْأَرْضِ وَلَنْ نُّعْجِزَهُ هَرَبًا ۝

9. We used, indeed, to sit there In (hidden) stations, to (steal) A hearing; but any who listens now Will find a flaming fire Watching him in ambush.

10. And we understand not Whether ill is intended to those on earth, Or whether their Lord (really) intends To guide them to right conduct.

11. There are among us some that are Righteous, and some the contrary: We follow divergent paths.

12. But we think that we can by no means Frustrate Allah throughout the earth, Nor can we frustrate Him by flight.

13. Wa annaa lammaa sami`-
nal-Hudaaa aamannaa bih.
Famany-yu'-mim-bi - Rabbihii
falaa yakhaafu bakh-sanw wa laa
rahaqaa.

١٣- وَّ اَنَّا لَمَّا سَمِعْنَا الْهُدٰٓى
اٰمَنَّا بِهٖ ؕ
فَمَنْ يُّؤْمِنْ بِرَبِّهٖ
فَلَا يَخَافُ بَخْسًا وَّ لَا رَهَقًا ○

14. Wa annaa minnal-Musli-
muuna wa minnal-Qaasituun.
Faman aslama fa-ulaaa-'ika
taharraw rashadaa.

١٤- وَّ اَنَّا مِنَّا الْمُسْلِمُوْنَ
وَ مِنَّا الْقٰسِطُوْنَ ؕ
فَمَنْ اَسْلَمَ فَاُولٰٓئِكَ
تَحَرَّوْا رَشَدًا ○

15. Wa ammal-Qaasituuna
fakaanuu li-Jahannama
hatabaa-

١٥- وَ اَمَّا الْقٰسِطُوْنَ فَكَانُوْا لِجَهَنَّمَ
حَطَبًا ○

13. And as for us, since we have listened To the guidance, we have accepted it: And any who believes in his Lord Has no fear, either of a short (account) Or of any injustice.

14. Amongst us are some That submit their wills (To Allah), and some That swerve from injustice. Now those who submit Their wills - they have Sought out (the path) Of right conduct

15. But those who swerve, They are (but) fuel for Hell-fire'

16. Wa alla-wist-taqaamuu alat - Tariiqati la - asqaynaa-hum-maa-'an ghadaqaa,

١٦- وَّاَنْ لَّوِاسْتَقَامُوْا
عَلَى الطَّرِيْقَةِ
لَاَسْقَيْنٰهُمْ مَّآءً غَدَقًا

17. Linaftinahum fiih. Wa many-yu`rid `an dhikri Rabbi-hii yasluk-hu `Adhaaban-sa-`adaa.

١٧- لِّنَفْتِنَهُمْ فِيْهِ
وَمَنْ يُّعْرِضْ عَنْ ذِكْرِ رَبِّهٖ
يَسْلُكْهُ عَذَابًا صَعَدًا

18. Wa annal-Masaajida lil-laahi falaa tad-`uu ma`a-Allaahi ahadaa;

١٨- وَّاَنَّ الْمَسٰجِدَ لِلّٰهِ
فَلَا تَدْعُوْا مَعَ اللّٰهِ اَحَدًا

19. Wa annahuu lammaa qaama `Abdullaahi yad-`uuhu kaaduu yakuunuuna `alay-hi libadaa.

١٩- وَّاَنَّهٗ لَمَّا قَامَ عَبْدُ اللّٰهِ يَدْعُوْهُ
كَادُوْا يَكُوْنُوْنَ عَلَيْهِ لِبَدًا

16. (And Allah's Message is) :" If they (the Pagans) Had (only) remained on the (right) Way, We should certainly have Bestowed on them Rain in abundance.

17. " That we might try them by that (means), But if any turns away from the remebrance Of his Lord, He will cause him to undergo A severe Penalty.

18. " And the places of worship are for Allah (alone): So invoke not anyone along with Allah;

19. " Yet when the devotee of Allah stands forth To invoke Him, they just Make round him a dense crowd. "

٢٠- قُلْ إِنَّمَآ أَدْعُوا
رَبِّي وَلَآ أُشْرِكُ بِهِۦٓ أَحَدًا ○

20. Qul innamaaa ad-`uu Rabbii wa laaa ushriku bihiii ahadaa.

٢١- قُلْ إِنِّي لَآ أَمْلِكُ
لَكُمْ ضَرًّا وَلَا رَشَدًا ○

21. Qul innii laa amliku lakum darranw-wa laa rashadaa.

٢٢- قُلْ إِنِّي لَن يُجِيرَنِي مِنَ ٱللَّهِ أَحَدٌ
وَلَنْ أَجِدَ مِن دُونِهِۦ مُلْتَحَدًا ○

22. Qul innii lany-yujiiranii mina-Allaahi ahadanw-wa lan min-duunihii mul-tahadaa,

٢٣- إِلَّا بَلَٰغًا مِّنَ ٱللَّهِ وَرِسَٰلَٰتِهِۦ
وَمَن يَعْصِ ٱللَّهَ وَرَسُولَهُۥ
فَإِنَّ لَهُۥ نَارَ جَهَنَّمَ
خَٰلِدِينَ فِيهَآ أَبَدًا ○

23. Illaa balaagham-mina-Allaahi wa Risaalaatih: wa many-ya`-sillaaha wa Rasuulahuu fa-inna lahuu Naara Jahannama khaalidiina fiihaaa abadaa.

20. Say: " I do no more than invoke my Lord, And I join not with Him any (false god). "

21. Say: " It is not in my power to cause You harm, or to bring you to right conduct. "

22. Say: " No one can deliver me from Allah (If I were to disobey Him) Nor should I find refuge except in Him,

23. " Unless I proclaim what I received From Allah And His Messages: For any that disobey Allah And His Messenger, - for them is Hell: They shall dwell therein for ever. "

24. Hattaaa i<u>dh</u>aa ra-'aw maa
yuu-`aduuna fa saya`-lamuuna
man ad-`afu naasiranw-wa
aqallu `adadaa.

٢٤- حَتّٰٓى إِذَا رَاَوْا مَا يُوْعَدُوْنَ
فَسَيَعْلَمُوْنَ مَنْ اَضْعَفُ نَاصِرًا
وَّاَقَلُّ عَدَدًا ○

25. Qul in-adriii a-qariibum-
maa tuu-`aduuna am yaj-`alu
lahuu Rabbiii amadaa.

٢٥- قُلْ إِنْ اَدْرِيْٓ
اَقَرِيْبٌ مَّا تُوْعَدُوْنَ
اَمْ يَجْعَلُ لَهٗ رَبِّيْٓ اَمَدًا ○

26. `Aalimul-<u>Gh</u>aybi falaa
yuzhiru `alaa <u>Gh</u>aybihiii
ahadaa,

٢٦- عٰلِمُ الْغَيْبِ
فَلَا يُظْهِرُ عَلٰى غَيْبِهٖٓ اَحَدًا ○

24. At length, when they see (with their own eyes) That which they are promised, Then will they know who it is that is Weakest in his (helper) And least important in point of numbers.

25. Say: "I know not whether the (punishment) Which you are promised is near, or whether My Lord will appoint for it a distant term.

26. " He (alone) knows the Unseen, Nor does He make anyone Acquainted with His Mysteries---

27. Illaa man-irtadaa mir-ra-
suulin-fa-innahuu yas-luku
mim-bayni yadayhi wa min
khalfihii rasadaa,

٢٧- إِلَّا مَنِ ارْتَضَىٰ مِن رَّسُولٍ
فَإِنَّهُ يَسْلُكُ
مِن بَيْنِ يَدَيْهِ وَمِنْ خَلْفِهِ رَصَدًا ۝

28. Li-ya`-lama an-qad abla-
ghuu Risaalaati Rabbihim wa
ahaata bimaa laday-him wa
'ahsaa kulla shay-'in `adadaa.

٢٨- لِّيَعْلَمَ
أَن قَدْ أَبْلَغُوا رِسَالَاتِ رَبِّهِمْ
وَأَحَاطَ بِمَا لَدَيْهِمْ
وَأَحْصَىٰ كُلَّ شَيْءٍ عَدَدًا ۝

27. " Except a Messenger whom He has chosen: And then He makes a band of watchers March before him and behind him.

28. " That he may know that they have (truly) Brought and delivered the Messages Of their Lord: And He surronds (All the mysteries) that are with them, And takes account of every single thing. "

سُورَةُ المُزَّمِّل

Al Muzzammil

جزء 29

Bisimillaahir - Rahmaanir - Rahiim. بِسْمِ اللّٰهِ الرَّحْمٰنِ الرَّحِيْمِ

1. Yaaa-ayyuhal - MUZZAM-MIL ! ١- يٰٓاَيُّهَا الْمُزَّمِّلُ ۙ

2. Qumil-layla illaa qalilaa, - ٢- قُمِ الَّيْلَ اِلَّا قَلِيْلًا ۙ

3. Nisfahuuu a-win-qus-minhu qaliilaa, ٣- نِّصْفَهٗٓ اَوِ انْقُصْ مِنْهُ قَلِيْلًا ۙ

4. Aw zid `alayhi wa rattilil-Qur-'aana tartiilaa. ٤- اَوْ زِدْ عَلَيْهِ وَرَتِّلِ الْقُرْاٰنَ تَرْتِيْلًا ۭ

5. Innaa sanulqii `alayka Qawlan-thaqiilaa. ٥- اِنَّا سَنُلْقِيْ عَلَيْكَ قَوْلًا ثَقِيْلًا

In the name of Allah, Most Gracious, Most Merciful.

1. O you folded in garments !

2. Stand (to pray) by night, but not all night,

3. Half of it, or a little less,

4. Or a little more; and recite the Qur'an In slow, measured rhythmic tones

5. Soon shall We send down To you a weighty Message.

6. Inna naashi-'atal-layli hiya ashaddu wat-anw-wa 'aqwa-mu Qiilaa.

٦-إِنَّ نَاشِئَةَ الَّيْلِ هِيَ أَشَدُّ وَطْأً
وَأَقْوَمُ قِيلًا ۝

7. Inna laka fin-nahaari sab-han-tawiilaa.

٧-إِنَّ لَكَ فِي النَّهَارِ
سَبْحًا طَوِيلًا ۝

8. Wadhkurisma Rabbika wa tabattal 'ilayhi tabtiilaa.

٨-وَاذْكُرِ اسْمَ رَبِّكَ
وَتَبَتَّلْ إِلَيْهِ تَبْتِيلًا ۝

9. Rabbul-Mashriqi wal-Magh-ribi Laaa ilaaha illaa Huwa fattakhidh-hu Wakiilaa.

٩-رَبُّ الْمَشْرِقِ وَالْمَغْرِبِ
لَا إِلَٰهَ إِلَّا هُوَ
فَاتَّخِذْهُ وَكِيلًا ۝

6. Truly the rising by night Is most potent for governing (The soul), and most suitable For (framing) the World (Of Prayer and Praise).

7. True, there is for you by day Prolonged occupation with ordinary duties:

8. But keep in remembrance the name Of your Lord and devote yourself To Him whole-heartedly.

9. (He is) Lord of the East and the West: There is no god but He: Take Him therefore For (your) Disposer of Affairs.

10. W'asbir `alaa maa yaquu-luuna w'ah-jurhum hajran-jamiilaa.

١٠- وَاصْبِرْ عَلَىٰ مَا يَقُولُونَ
وَاهْجُرْهُمْ هَجْرًا جَمِيلًا ۝

11. Wa dharnii wal-mukadh-dhi-biina ulin-na`-mati wa mah-hil-hum qaliilaa.

١١- وَذَرْنِي
وَالْمُكَذِّبِينَ أُولِي النَّعْمَةِ
وَمَهِّلْهُمْ قَلِيلًا ۝

12. Inna ladaynaaa ankaa-lanw-wa Jahiimaa,

١٢- إِنَّ لَدَيْنَا أَنكَالًا وَجَحِيمًا ۝

13. Wa Ta-`aaman-dhaa ghussa-tinw-wa `Adhaaban aliimaa.

١٣- وَطَعَامًا ذَا غُصَّةٍ
وَعَذَابًا أَلِيمًا ۝

10. And have patience with what they say, And leave them with noble (dignity).

11. And leave Me (alone to deal with) Those in possession of the good things of life, Who (yet) deny the Truth; And bear with them for a little while.

12. With Us are Fetters (to bind them), And a Fire (to burn them),

13. And a food that chokes, And a Penalty Grievous.

14. Yawma tarjuful-ardu wal-
jibaalu wa kaanatil - jibaalu
kathiibam-mahiilaa.

١٤- يَوْمَ تَرْجُفُ الْأَرْضُ وَالْجِبَالُ
وَكَانَتِ الْجِبَالُ
كَثِيبًا مَّهِيلًا ۝

15. Innaaa arsalnaaa ilaykum
Rasuulan-shaahidan `alaykum
kamaaa arsalnaaa ilaa Fir-
`awna Rasuulaa.

١٥- إِنَّا أَرْسَلْنَا إِلَيْكُمْ رَسُولًا ۥ
شَاهِدًا عَلَيْكُمْ
كَمَا أَرْسَلْنَا إِلَىٰ فِرْعَوْنَ رَسُولًا ۝

16. Fa-`asaa Fir-`awnur-Rasuu-
la fa-akhadhnaahu akhdhanw-
wabiilaa.

١٦- فَعَصَىٰ فِرْعَوْنُ الرَّسُولَ
فَأَخَذْنَاهُ أَخْذًا وَبِيلًا ۝

17. Fakay-fa tattaquuna in-
kafartum Yawmany - yaj-`alul-
wildaana shiibaa -

١٧- فَكَيْفَ تَتَّقُونَ إِن كَفَرْتُمْ
يَوْمًا يَجْعَلُ الْوِلْدَانَ شِيبًا ۝

14. One day the earth and the mountains Will be in violent commotion, and The mountains will be as a heap of sand Poured out and flowing down.

15. We have sent to you, (o men !) a Messenger, To be a witness concerning you, Even as We sent a Messenger to Pharaoh.

16. But Pharaoh disobeyed the Messenger; So We seized him with a heavy punishment.

17. Then how shall you, if you deny (Allah), Guard yourselves against a Day that will make Children hoary-headed ?

18. As-samaaa-'u munfatirum-
bih ? Kaana wa`-duhuu maf-
`uulaa.

١٨- السَّمَآءُ مُنْفَطِرٌۢ بِهٖ ط
كَانَ وَعْدُهٗ مَفْعُوْلًا ○

19. Inna haadhihii Tadhkirah:
faman shaaa-'attakhadha ilaa
Rabbihii Sabiilaa !

١٩- اِنَّ هٰذِهٖ تَذْكِرَةٌ ج
فَمَنْ شَآءَ اتَّخَذَ اِلٰى رَبِّهٖ سَبِيْلًا ○

20. Inna Rabbaka ya`-lamu
annaka taquumu adnaa min-
thuluthayil-layli wa nisfahuu wa
thuluthahuu wa taaa-'ifatum-mi-
nalladhiina ma-`ak. w-Allaahuu
yuqaddirul - layla wan-nahaar.
`Alima allan-tuhsuuhu fataaba
`alay-kum faq-ra-'uu maa ta-

٢٠- اِنَّ رَبَّكَ يَعْلَمُ اَنَّكَ تَقُوْمُ اَدْنٰى
مِنْ ثُلُثَيِ الَّيْلِ وَنِصْفَهٗ
وَثُلُثَهٗ وَطَآئِفَةٌ مِّنَ الَّذِيْنَ مَعَكَ ط
وَاللّٰهُ يُقَدِّرُ الَّيْلَ وَالنَّهَارَ ط
عَلِمَ اَنْ لَّنْ تُحْصُوْهُ
فَتَابَ عَلَيْكُمْ
فَاقْرَءُوْا

18. Whereon the sky will be cleft asunder ? His Promise needs must be accomplished.

19. Verily this is an Admonition: Therefore, whoso will, let him Take a (straight) path to his Lord !

20. The Lord does know that you stand forth To (prayer) nigh two-thirds of the night, Or half the night or a third of the night, And so does a party of those with you, But Allah does appoint Night And day in due measure. He knows that you are Unable to keep account thereof So He Has turned to you (in mercy): Read

مَا تَيَسَّرَ مِنَ الْقُرْاٰنِ ؕ
عَلِمَ اَنْ سَيَكُوْنُ مِنْكُمْ مَّرْضٰى ۙ
وَاٰخَرُوْنَ يَضْرِبُوْنَ فِى الْاَرْضِ
يَبْتَغُوْنَ مِنْ فَضْلِ اللّٰهِ ۙ
وَاٰخَرُوْنَ يُقَاتِلُوْنَ فِىْ سَبِيْلِ اللّٰهِ ۖ
فَاقْرَءُوْا مَا تَيَسَّرَ مِنْهُ ۙ
وَاَقِيْمُوا الصَّلٰوةَ وَاٰتُوا الزَّكٰوةَ
وَاَقْرِضُوا اللّٰهَ قَرْضًا حَسَنًا ؕ
وَمَا تُقَدِّمُوْا لِاَنْفُسِكُمْ مِّنْ خَيْرٍ
تَجِدُوْهُ عِنْدَ اللّٰهِ
هُوَ خَيْرًا وَّاَعْظَمَ اَجْرًا ؕ
وَاسْتَغْفِرُوا اللّٰهَ ؕ
اِنَّ اللّٰهَ غَفُوْرٌ رَّحِيْمٌ ۝

yassara minal-Qur-'aan. `Alima an-sayakuunu minkum-mardaa wa 'aakharuuna yadribuuna fil-ardi yabtaghuuna min-Fadlillaahi wa aakharuuna yuqaatiluuna fii Sabiilillaah. F'aqra-'uu maa tayassara minhu wa aqimmus-Salaata wa aatuz-Zakaata wa aqridul-laaha Qardan Hasanna. Wa maa tuqaddimuu li-anfusikum-min khay-rin-tajiduuhu `'indal-laahi huwa khay-ranw-wa A`-zama Ajraa. Wastaghfirul-laah: innallaaha Ghafuurur-Rahiim.

you therefore, fo the Qur'an As much as may beeasy for you. He knows that there may be (some) Among you in ill-health; Others travelling through the land, Seeking of Allah's bounty; Yet others fighting in Allah's Cause. Read you, therefore, as much of the Qur'an As may be easy (for you); And establish regular Prayer And give regular Charity (zakah) ;And loan to Allah a Beautiful Loan.

And whatever good you send forth For your souls, you shall find it In Allah's Presence, yea, better and Greater in Reward. And seek you the Grace of Allah: For Allah is oft-Forgiving, Most Merciful.

سُورَةُ المدَّثِّر

Al Muddaththir

جزء 29

Bismillaahir - Rahmaanir - Rahiim. بِسْمِ اللّٰهِ الرَّحْمٰنِ الرَّحِيْمِ

1. Yaaa-ayyuhal-MUDDATH-THIR ! ١-يَاَيُّهَا الْمُدَّثِّرُ ۝

2. Qum fa-andhir ! ٢-قُمْ فَاَنْذِرْ ۝

3. Wa Rabbaka fa-kabbir ! ٣-وَرَبَّكَ فَكَبِّرْ ۝

4. Wa thiyaabaka fatahhir ! ٤-وَثِيَابَكَ فَطَهِّرْ ۝

5. Warrujza fahjur ! ٥-وَالرُّجْزَ فَاهْجُرْ ۝

6. Wa laa tamnun-tastaksir. ٦-وَلَا تَمْنُنْ تَسْتَكْثِرُ ۝

7. Wa li-Rabbika fasbir ! ٧-وَلِرَبِّكَ فَاصْبِرْ ۝

In the name of Allah, Most Gracious, Most Merciful

1. O you wrapped up (in a mantle) !

2. Arise and deliver your warning !

3. And your Lord do you magnify !

4. And your garments keep free from stain !

5. And all abomination shun !

6. Nor expect, in giving, Any increase (for yourself) !

7. But, for your Lord's (Cause), Be patient and constant !

8. Fa-idhaa nuqira fin-naaquur,	٨- فَإِذَا نُقِرَ فِي النَّاقُورِ ۝
9. Fa-dhaalika Yawma-'idhiny-Yawnun 'asiir,	٩- فَذَٰلِكَ يَوْمَئِذٍ يَوْمٌ عَسِيرٌ ۝
10. \`Alal-kaafiriina ghayru yasiir	١٠- عَلَى الْكَافِرِينَ غَيْرُ يَسِيرٍ ۝
11. Dharnii wa man khalaqtu wahiidaa ! -	١١- ذَرْنِي وَمَنْ خَلَقْتُ وَحِيدًا ۝
12. Wa ja-\`altu lahuu maalam-mamduudaa,	١٢- وَجَعَلْتُ لَهُ مَالًا مَمْدُودًا ۝
13. Wa baniina shuhuudaa !	١٣- وَبَنِينَ شُهُودًا ۝
14. Wa mahhattu lahuu tamhiidaa !	١٤- وَمَهَّدْتُ لَهُ تَمْهِيدًا ۝

8. Finally, when the trumpet is sounded,

9. That will be -that day -a Day of Distress, -

10. Far from easy for those wiyout Faith

11. Leave Me alone, (to deal) With the (creature) whom I created (bare and) alone !

12, To whom I granted resources in abundance,

13. And sons to be by his side !

14. To whom I made (Life) smooth and comfortable !

15. Thumma yatma-`u an aziid;

١٥- ثُمَّ يَطْمَعُ اَنْ اَزِيْدَ ۙ

16. Kallaa ! innahuu kaana li-Aayaatinaa `aniidaa !

١٦- كَلَّا ؕ اِنَّهٗ كَانَ لِاٰيٰتِنَا عَنِيْدًا ؕ

17. Sa-'urhiquhuu sa-`uudaa !

١٧- سَاُرْهِقُهٗ صَعُوْدًا ؕ

18. Innahuu fakkara wa qaddar;

١٨- اِنَّهٗ فَكَّرَ وَ قَدَّرَ ۙ

19. Faqutila kayfa qaddar !

١٩- فَقُتِلَ كَيْفَ قَدَّرَ ۙ

20. Thumma qutila kayfa qad-dar !

٢٠- ثُمَّ قُتِلَ كَيْفَ قَدَّرَ ۙ

21. Thumma nazar;

٢١- ثُمَّ نَظَرَ ۙ

15. Yet is he greedy -that I should add (yet more);

16. By no means ? for to Our signs He has been refractory !

17. Soon will I visit him With a mount of calamaties !

18. For he thought and he plotted;

19. And woe to him ! how he plotted ! -

20. Yea, woe to him ! how he plotted ! -

21. Then he looked round;

22. Thumma `abasa wa basar;
۲۲-ثُمَّ عَبَسَ وَبَسَرَ ۝

23. Thumma adbara wastakbar;
۲۳-ثُمَّ أَدْبَرَ وَاسْتَكْبَرَ ۝

24. Faqaala in haadhaaa illaa sihruny-yu'-thar;
۲۴-فَقَالَ
إِنْ هَٰذَآ إِلَّا سِحْرٌ يُؤْثَرُ ۝

25. In haadhaaa illaa qawlul bashar !
۲۵-إِنْ هَٰذَآ إِلَّا قَوْلُ الْبَشَرِ ۝

26. Sa-'usliihi Saqar !
۲۶-سَأُصْلِيهِ سَقَرَ ۝

27. Wa maaa adraaka maa Saqar ?
۲۷-وَمَآ أَدْرَاكَ مَا سَقَرُ ۝

22. Then he frowned and he scowled;

23. Then he turned back and was haughty;

24. Then said he:" This is nothing but magic, Derived from of old;

25. " This is nothing but the word of a mortal ! "

26. Soon will I cast him into Hell-Fire !

27. And what will explain To you what Hell-Fire is ?

٢٨- لَا تُبْقِي وَلَا تَذَرُ

28. Laa tubqii wa laa ta<u>dh</u>ar !

٢٩- لَوَّاحَةٌ لِّلْبَشَرِ

29. Lawwaahatul-lil-ba<u>sh</u>ar !

٣٠- عَلَيْهَا تِسْعَةَ عَشَرَ

30. `Alayhaa tis-`ata `ashar

٣١- وَمَا جَعَلْنَا أَصْحَابَ النَّارِ إِلَّا مَلَائِكَةً
وَمَا جَعَلْنَا عِدَّتَهُمْ إِلَّا فِتْنَةً
لِّلَّذِينَ كَفَرُوا لِيَسْتَيْقِنَ الَّذِينَ أُوتُوا
الْكِتَابَ وَيَزْدَادَ الَّذِينَ آمَنُوا إِيمَانًا
وَلَا يَرْتَابَ الَّذِينَ أُوتُوا الْكِتَابَ وَالْمُؤْمِنُونَ

31. Wa maa ja-`alnaaa As-haabannaari illaa malaaa-'i-kah. Wa maa ja-`alnaa `iddata-hum illaa fitnatal-lilla<u>dh</u>iina kafaruu li-yastay-qinalla<u>dh</u>iina uutul-Kitaaba wa yazdaadal-la<u>dh</u>iina aamanuuu iimaananw-wa laa yartaaballa<u>dh</u>iina uutul-Kitaaba wal-Mu`-minuuna wa

28. It does not permit To endure, and nor does it leave alone ! -

29. Darkening and changing the color of man !

30. Over it are Nineteen.

31. And We have set none But angels as guardians of the Fire; And We have fixed their number Only as a trial for Unbelievers, - In order. That the People of the Book May arrive at certainty, And the Believers may increaseiIn Faith - And that no doubts

li-yaquulalladhiina fii quluubi-him - maradunw-wal-kaafiruuna maa - dhaa araadallaahu bi-haadhaa mathalaa ? Kadhaalika yudillullaahu many-yashaaa-'u wa yahdi many-yashaaa'. Wa maa ya`-lamu junuuda Rabbika illaa Huu. Wa maa hiya illaa dhikraa lil-bashar.

وَلِيَقُوْلَ الَّذِيْنَ فِيْ قُلُوْبِهِمْ مَّرَضٌ
وَّالْكٰفِرُوْنَ مَاذَآ اَرَادَ اللّٰهُ بِهٰذَا مَثَلًا ؕ
كَذٰلِكَ يُضِلُّ اللّٰهُ مَنْ يَّشَآءُ
وَيَهْدِيْ مَنْ يَّشَآءُ ؕ
وَمَا يَعْلَمُ جُنُوْدَ رَبِّكَ اِلَّا هُوَ ؕ
وَمَا هِيَ اِلَّا ذِكْرٰى لِلْبَشَرِ ۧ

32. Kallaa wal-Qamar,

٣٢-كَلَّا وَالْقَمَرِ ۙ

33. Wallayli idh adbar,

٣٣-وَالَّيْلِ اِذْ اَدْبَرَ ۙ

34. Was-Subhi idhaa asfar,

٣٤-وَالصُّبْحِ اِذَآ اَسْفَرَ ۙ

May be left for the People Of the Book and the Believers, And that those in whose hearts Is a disease and the Unbelievers May say, " What symbol Does Allah intend by this ? " Thus does Allah leave to stray Whom He pleases, and guide Whom He pleases: and none can know the forces

Of the Lord, except He, and this is no other than A warning to mankind.

32. Nay, verily: By the Moon,

33. And by the Night as it retreats,

34. And by the Dawn as it shines forth,

35. Innahaa la-'ihdal-kubar, ٣٥-إِنَّهَا لَإِحْدَى الْكُبَرِ ۝

36. Nadhiral-lil-bashar, ٣٦-نَذِيرًا لِّلْبَشَرِ ۝

37. Liman shaaa-'a minkum any-yata-qaddama aw yata-'akh-khar; ٣٧-لِمَن شَاءَ مِنكُمْ أَن يَتَقَدَّمَ أَوْ يَتَأَخَّرَ ۝

38. Kullu nafsim-bimaa kasa-bat rahiinah, ٣٨-كُلُّ نَفْسٍ بِمَا كَسَبَتْ رَهِينَةٌ ۝

39. Illaaa As-haabal-yamiin. ٣٩-إِلَّا أَصْحَابَ الْيَمِينِ ۝

40. Fii Jannaatiny-yatasaaa-'aluun ٤٠-فِي جَنَّاتٍ يَتَسَاءَلُونَ ۝

35. This is but one of the mighty (portents),

36. A warning to mankind, -

37. To any of you that chooses To press forward, or to follow behind.

38. Every soul will be (held) In pledge for its deeds.

39. Except the Companions of the Right Hand,

40. (They will be) in Gardens (of Delight): They will question each other,

41. `Anil-mujrimiin : ۴۱- عَنِ الْمُجْرِمِيْنَ ۝

42. Maa salakakum fii Saqar ? ۴۲- مَا سَلَكَكُمْ فِيْ سَقَرَ ۝

43. Qaaluu lam naku minal-Musalliin; ۴۳- قَالُوْا لَمْ نَكُ مِنَ الْمُصَلِّيْنَ ۝

44. Wa lam naku nut-`imul-Miskiin ; ۴۴- وَلَمْ نَكُ نُطْعِمُ الْمِسْكِيْنَ ۝

45. Wa kunnaa nakhuudu ma-`al-khaaa-'idiin; ۴۵- وَكُنَّا نَخُوْضُ مَعَ الْخَآئِضِيْنَ ۝

46. Wa kunnaa nukadh-dh-ibu bi-Yawmid-Diin ۴۶- وَكُنَّا نُكَذِّبُ بِيَوْمِ الدِّيْنِ ۝

47. Hattaaa ataanal-yaqiin. ۴۷- حَتّٰى اَتٰنَا الْيَقِيْنُ ۝

41. And (ask) of the Sinners:

42. " What led you into Hell-Fire ? "

43. They will say: " We were not of those Who prayed;

44. " Nor we of those who fed the indigent:

45. " But we used to talk Vanities with vain talkers;

46. " And we used to deny The Day of Judgement

47. " Until there came to us (The Hour) that is Certain. "

48. Famaa tanfa-`uhum shafaa-`atush-shaafi-`iin.

٤٨-فَمَا تَنفَعُهُمْ شَفَاعَةُ الشَّفِعِينَ ۝

49. Famaa lahum `anit-tadhki-rati mu`-ridiin.

٤٩-فَمَا لَهُمْ عَنِ
التَّذْكِرَةِ مُعْرِضِينَ ۝

50. Ka-'annahum humurum-mustanfirah

٥٠-كَأَنَّهُمْ حُمُرٌ مُّسْتَنفِرَةٌ ۝

51. Farrat min-qaswarah !

٥١-فَرَّتْ مِن قَسْوَرَةٍ ۝

52. Bal yuriidu kullum-ri-'im-minhum any-yu 'taa suhufam-munash-sharah !

٥٢-بَلْ يُرِيدُ كُلُّ امْرِئٍ مِّنْهُمْ
أَن يُؤْتَى صُحُفًا مُّنَشَّرَةً ۝

48. Then will no intercession Of (any) intercessors profit them.

49. Then what is the matter with them That they turn away Ffom admonition ?-

50. As if they were affrighted asses,

51. Fleeing from a lion !

52. Forsooth, each one of them Wants to be given Scrolls (of revelation) spread out !

٥٣- كَلَّا ۖ بَل لَّا يَخَافُونَ الْآخِرَةَ ۝

53. Kallaa ! Bal laa yakhaa-fuunal-Aakhirah.

٥٤- كَلَّا إِنَّهُ تَذْكِرَةٌ ۝

54. Kallaa innahuu tadhkirah:

٥٥- فَمَن شَاءَ ذَكَرَهُ ۝

55. Faman-shaaa-'a dhakarah !

٥٦- وَمَا يَذْكُرُونَ إِلَّا أَن يَشَاءَ اللَّهُ ۚ
هُوَ أَهْلُ التَّقْوَىٰ
وَأَهْلُ الْمَغْفِرَةِ ۝

56. Wa maa yadhkuruuna illaaa any-yashaaa -Allaah: Huwa Ahlut-taqwaa wa Ahlul-Maghfirah.

53. By no means ! But They fear not the Hereafter.

54. Nay, this surely is an admonition

55. Let any who will, Keep it in remembrance !

56. But none will keep it In remembrance except as Allah wills: He is the Lord of Righteousness, And the Lord of Forgiveness.

سورة القيامة

Al Qiyānah

جزء 29

Bismillaahir - Rahmaanir - Rahiim. بِسْمِ اللّٰهِ الرَّحْمٰنِ الرَّحِيْمِ

1. Laa uqsimu bi-Yawmil-QIYAAMAH; ١- لَآ اُقْسِمُ بِيَوْمِ الْقِيٰمَةِ ۝

2. Wa laa uqsimu bin-nafsil-lawwaamah. ٢- وَلَآ اُقْسِمُ بِالنَّفْسِ اللَّوَّامَةِ ۝

3. Ayahsabul-insaanu allan-najma-`a `izaamah ? ٣- اَيَحْسَبُ الْاِنْسَانُ اَلَّنْ نَّجْمَعَ عِظَامَهٗ ۝

4. Balaa Qaadiriina `alaaa an-nusawwiya banaanah. ٤- بَلٰى قٰدِرِيْنَ عَلٰٓى اَنْ نُّسَوِّيَ بَنَانَهٗ ۝

5. Bal yuriidul-'Insaanu li-yaf-jura amaamah. ٥- بَلْ يُرِيْدُ الْاِنْسَانُ لِيَفْجُرَ اَمَامَهٗ ۝

In the name of Allah, Most Gracious, Most Merciful.

1. I do call to witness the Resurrection Day;

2. And I do call to witness The self-reproaching spirit: (Eschew Evil).

3. Does man think that We cannot assemble his bones ?

4. Nay, We are able to put together in perfect order The very tips of his fingers.

5. But man wishes to do wrong (even) in the time In front of him.

6. Yas-'alu ayyaana Yawmul-Qiyaamah ?

٦- يَسْـَٔلُ أَيَّانَ يَوْمُ الْقِيٰمَةِ ۝

7. Fa-idhaa bariqal-basar,

٧- فَإِذَا بَرِقَ الْبَصَرُ ۝

8. Wa khasafal-Qamar.

٨- وَخَسَفَ الْقَمَرُ ۝

9. Wa jumi-`ash-shamsu wal-qamar,

٩- وَجُمِعَ الشَّمْسُ وَالْقَمَرُ ۝

10. Yaquulul-'insaanu Yawma-'idhin aynal-mafarr ?

١٠- يَقُولُ الْإِنْسَانُ يَوْمَئِذٍ أَيْنَ الْمَفَرُّ ۝

11. Kallaa laa wazar !

١١- كَلَّا لَا وَزَرَ ۝

12. Ilaa Rabbika Yawma-'idhi-nil-mustaqarr.

١٢- إِلَىٰ رَبِّكَ يَوْمَئِذٍ الْمُسْتَقَرُّ ۝

6. He questions: " When is the Day of Resurrection ? "

7. At length, when the Sight is dazed.

8. And the moon is buried in darkness,

9. And the sun and moon are joined together,

10. That Day will Man say: " Where is the refuge ? "

11. By no means ! No place of safety !

12. Before your Lord (alone), That Day will be the place of rest.

13. Yunnabba-'ul-insaanu Yaw-ma-'idhim-bimaa qaddama wa akh-khar.

١٣- يُنَبَّؤُا الْإِنْسَانُ يَوْمَئِذٍ بِمَا قَدَّمَ وَأَخَّرَ ۝

14. Balil-'insaanu `alaa nafsihii basiirah,

١٤- بَلِ الْإِنْسَانُ عَلَىٰ نَفْسِهِ بَصِيرَةٌ ۝

15. Wa law alqaa ma-`aadhiirah.

١٥- وَلَوْ أَلْقَىٰ مَعَاذِيرَهُ ۝

16. Laa tuharrik bihii lisaanaka li-ta`-jala bih.

١٦- لَا تُحَرِّكْ بِهِ لِسَانَكَ لِتَعْجَلَ بِهِ ۝

17. Inna `alaynaa jam-`ahuu wa qur-'aanah:

١٧- إِنَّ عَلَيْنَا جَمْعَهُ وَقُرْآنَهُ ۝

18. Fa-'idhaa qara'-naahu fat-tabi` qur-'aanah:

١٨- فَإِذَا قَرَأْنَاهُ فَاتَّبِعْ قُرْآنَهُ ۝

13. That Day will Man be told (all) that he Put forward, and all that hc put back.

14. Nay, man will be evidence against himself,

15. Even though he were to put up his excuses.

16. Move not your tongue concerning The (Qur'an) to make haste therewith.

17. It is for us to collect it And to promulgate it:

18. But when We have promulgated it, Follow you its recital (as promulgated):

19. <u>Th</u>umma inna \`alaynaa bayaanah:	۱۹-ثُمَّ إِنَّ عَلَيْنَا بَيَانَهُ ۝
20. Kalla bal tuhibbuunal-\`aa-jilah,	۲۰-كَلَّا بَلْ تُحِبُّونَ الْعَاجِلَةَ ۝
21. Wa ta<u>dh</u>aruunal-A<u>akh</u>irah.	۲۱-وَتَذَرُونَ الْآخِرَةَ ۝
22. Wujuuhuny-Yawma-i<u>dh</u>in-naadirah;	۲۲-وُجُوهٌ يَوْمَئِذٍ نَاضِرَةٌ ۝
23. Ilaa Rabbihaa naazirah;	۲۳-إِلَىٰ رَبِّهَا نَاظِرَةٌ ۝
24. Wa wujuuhuny-Yawma-i<u>dh</u>im-baasirah,	۲۴-وَوُجُوهٌ يَوْمَئِذٍ بَاسِرَةٌ ۝
25. Tazunnu any-yuf-\`ala bi-haa faaqirah;	۲۵-تَظُنُّ أَنْ يُفْعَلَ بِهَا فَاقِرَةٌ ۝

19. Nay more, it is for Us to explain it (And make it clear):

20. Nay, (you men !) but you love The fleeting life,

21. And leave alone the Hereafter.

22. Some faces that day, Will beam (in brightness and beauty);

23. Looking towards their Lord;

24. And some faces, that Day, Will be sad and dismal,

25. In the thought that some Back-breaking calamity was about To be inflicted on them;

26. Kallaaa idhaa balaghatit-taraaqii, ٢٦- كَلَّآ إِذَا بَلَغَتِ التَّرَاقِيَ ۝

27. Wa qiila man - raaq ? ٢٧- وَقِيلَ مَنْ ۜ رَاقٍ ۝

28. Wa zanna annahul-firaaq; ٢٨- وَّظَنَّ أَنَّهُ الْفِرَاقُ ۝

29. Wal-taffatis-saaqu bis-saaq: ٢٩- وَالْتَفَّتِ السَّاقُ بِالسَّاقِ ۝

30. Ilaa Rabbika Yawma-'idhi-nil-maasaaq ! ٣٠- إِلَىٰ رَبِّكَ يَوْمَئِذٍ الْمَسَاقُ ۝

31. Falaa saddaqa wa laa sallaa ! ٣١- فَلَا صَدَّقَ وَلَا صَلَّىٰ ۝

32. Wa laakin-kadh-dhaba wa tawallaa ! ٣٢- وَلَٰكِن كَذَّبَ وَتَوَلَّىٰ ۝

26. Yea, when (the soul) Reaches to the collar-bone (in its exit).

27. And there will be a cry, " Who is a magician (to restore him)

28. And he will conclude That it was (the Time) of Parting;

29. And one leg will be joined with another:

30. That Day the Drive Will be (all) to your Lord !

31. So he gave nothing in charity, nor Did he pray !

32. But on the contrary he rejected Truth And turned away !

33. <u>Th</u>umma dhahaba ilaaa ah-lihii yatamattaa !

۳۳-ثُمَّ ذَهَبَ إِلَىٰٓ أَهْلِهٖ يَتَمَطّٰىٓ ۝

34. Awlaa laka fa-'awlaa !

۳۴-أَوْلٰى لَكَ فَأَوْلٰى ۝

35. <u>Th</u>umma 'awlaa laka fa-'awlaa !

۳۵-ثُمَّ أَوْلٰى لَكَ فَأَوْلٰىٓ ۝

36. A-yahsabul-insaanu any-yutraka sudaa ?

۳۶-أَيَحْسَبُ الْإِنْسَانُ أَنْ يُّتْرَكَ سُدًى ۝

37. Alam yaku nutfatam-mim-maniy-yiny-yumnaa ?

۳۷-أَلَمْ يَكُ نُطْفَةً
مِّنْ مَّنِيٍّ يُّمْنٰى ۝

33. Then did he stalk to his family In full conceit !

34. Woe to you, (o man !), yea, woe !

35. Again, woe to you, (o man!), yea, woe !

36. Does man think that he will be left Uncontrolled, (without purpose) ?

37. Was he not a drop of sperm emitted (In lowly form) ?

38. Thumma kaana `alaqatan-fa-khalaqa fasawwaa.

٣٨- ثُمَّ كَانَ عَلَقَةً
فَخَلَقَ فَسَوّٰى ۝

39. Faja-`ala minhuz-zaw-jay-niz-dhakara wal-'unthaa.

٣٩- فَجَعَلَ مِنْهُ الزَّوْجَيْنِ
الذَّكَرَ وَالْاُنْثٰى ۝

40. Alaysa dhaalika bi-qaadirin `alaaa any-yuh-yiyal-mawtaa ?

٤٠- اَلَيْسَ ذٰلِكَ بِقٰدِرٍ
عَلٰٓى اَنْ يُّحْيِۦَ الْمَوْتٰى ۝

38. Then did he become a leech-like clot; Then did (Allah) mak and fashion (him) In due proportion.

39. And of him He made two sexes, Male and female.

40. Has not He, (the same), The power to give life to the dead ?

سُوْرَةُ الدَّهر

Al Dahr

جزء 29

Bismillaahir - Rahmaanir - Rahiim. بِسْمِ اللّٰهِ الرَّحْمٰنِ الرَّحِيْمِ

1. Hal ataa `alal-INSAANI hiinum-minad-DAHRI lam yakun-shay-'am-madhkuuraa ?

١- هَلْ اَتٰى عَلَى الْاِنْسَانِ حِيْنٌ مِّنَ الدَّهْرِ لَمْ يَكُنْ شَيْئًا مَّذْكُوْرًا ○

2. Innaa khalaqnal-insaana min - nutfatin amshaajin-nabtaliihi faja-`alnaahu samii-`am-basiiraa.

٢- اِنَّا خَلَقْنَا الْاِنْسَانَ مِنْ نُّطْفَةٍ اَمْشَاجٍ نَّبْتَلِيْهِ فَجَعَلْنٰهُ سَمِيْعًا بَصِيْرًا ○

3. Innaa haday-naahus-sabiila immaa shaakiranw-wa immaa kafuuraa.

٣- اِنَّا هَدَيْنٰهُ السَّبِيْلَ اِمَّا شَاكِرًا وَّ اِمَّا كَفُوْرًا ○

4. Innaaa a`-tadnaa lil-kaafi-riina salaasila wa aghlaalanw-wa sa-`iiraa.

٤- اِنَّآ اَعْتَدْنَا لِلْكٰفِرِيْنَ سَلٰسِلَاْ وَاَغْلٰلًا وَّسَعِيْرًا ○

In the name of Allah, Most Gracious, Most Merciful.

1. Has there not been over Man A long period of Time, when he was Nothing - (not even) mentioned ?

2. Verily We created man from a drop Of mingled sperm, In order to try him so we gave him (the gifts) Of Hearing and Sight.

3. We showed him the Way: Whether he be grateful or ungrateful (Rests on his will).

4. For the Rejecters We have prepared Chains, Yokes, and a Blazing Fire.

٥-إِنَّ الْأَبْرَارَ يَشْرَبُونَ
مِن كَأْسٍ كَانَ مِزَاجُهَا كَافُورًا ۝

5. Innal abraara yashrabuuna min-ka'-sin-kaana mizaajuhaa kaafuuraa,

٦-عَيْنًا يَشْرَبُ بِهَا عِبَادُ اللَّهِ
يُفَجِّرُونَهَا تَفْجِيرًا ۝

6. `Ayany - yash - rabu bihaa `Ibaadullaahi yufajji-ruunahaa taf-jiiraa.

٧-يُوفُونَ بِالنَّذْرِ
وَيَخَافُونَ يَوْمًا كَانَ شَرُّهُ مُسْتَطِيرًا ۝

7. Yuufuuna binnadhri wa ya-khaafuuna yawman-kaana sharrahuu musta-tiiraa.

٨-وَيُطْعِمُونَ الطَّعَامَ عَلَىٰ حُبِّهِ مِسْكِينًا
وَيَتِيمًا وَأَسِيرًا ۝

8. Wa yut-`imuunat-ta-`aama `alaa hubbihii miskiinanw-wa yatiimanw-wa 'asiiraa, -

٩-إِنَّمَا نُطْعِمُكُمْ لِوَجْهِ اللَّهِ
لَا نُرِيدُ مِنكُمْ جَزَاءً وَلَا شُكُورًا ۝

9. Innamaa nut-`imukum li-waj-hillaahi laa nuriidu min-kum jazaaa-'anw-wa laa shu-kuuraa.

5. As to the Righteous, they shall drink Of a Cup (of Wine) Mixed with *Kafur*

6. A Fountain where the Devotees of Allah Do drink, making it flow in unstinted abundance.

7. They perform (their) vows and they fear a Day Whose evil flies far and wide.

8. And they feed, for the love of Allah, The indigent, the orphan, and the captive,

9. (Saying), " We feed youfFor the sake of Allah alone: No reward do we desire From you, nor thanks.

10. Inaa nakhaafu mir-Rabbinaa Yawman `abuusan-qamtariiraa.

١٠- إِنَّا نَخَافُ مِن رَّبِّنَا
يَوْمًا عَبُوسًا قَمْطَرِيرًا ○

11. Fawaqaahumullaahu sharra dhaalikal-Yawmi wa laqqaahum nazratanw-wa suruuraa.

١١- فَوَقَاهُمُ اللَّهُ شَرَّ ذَٰلِكَ الْيَوْمِ
وَلَقَّاهُمْ نَضْرَةً
وَسُرُورًا ○

12. Wa jazaahum-bimaa sabaruu Jannatanw-wa hariiraa.

١٢- وَجَزَاهُم بِمَا صَبَرُوا
جَنَّةً وَحَرِيرًا ○

13. Muttaki-'iina fiihaa `alal-araaa-'ik, laa yarawna fiiha shamsanw-wa laa zam-hariiraa.

١٣- مُّتَّكِئِينَ فِيهَا عَلَى الْأَرَائِكِ ۖ
لَا يَرَوْنَ فِيهَا شَمْسًا
وَلَا زَمْهَرِيرًا ○

10. " We only fear a Day of distressful Wrath From the side of our Lord."

11. " But Allah will deliver them from the evil Of that Day, and will shed over them a Light Of Beauty and a (blissful) Joy.

12. And because they were patient and constant, He will Reward them with a Garden And (garments of) silk,

13. Reclining in the (Garden) on raised thrones, They will see there neither The sun's (excessive heat) Nor (the moon's) excessive cold,

14. Wa daaniyatan `alay-him zilaaluhaa wa dhulli-lat qutuu-fuhaa tadh-liilaa.

١٤- وَدَانِيَةً عَلَيْهِمْ ظِلَالُهَا
وَذُلِّلَتْ قُطُوفُهَا تَذْلِيلًا ○

15. Wa yutaafu `alay-him-bi-'aaniyatim - min - fiddatinw-wa 'ak - waabin-kaanat qawaarii-raa,

١٥- وَيُطَافُ عَلَيْهِم بِآنِيَةٍ مِّن فِضَّةٍ
وَأَكْوَابٍ كَانَتْ قَوَارِيرَا ○

16. Qawaariira min-fiddatin-qaddaruuhaa taqdiiraa.

١٦- قَوَارِيرَا مِن فِضَّةٍ
قَدَّرُوهَا تَقْدِيرًا ○

17. Wa yus-qawna fiihaa ka'-san-kaana mizaajuhaa zanjbiilaa,

١٧- وَيُسْقَوْنَ فِيهَا كَأْسًا
كَانَ مِزَاجُهَا زَنجَبِيلًا ○

18. `Ay-nan-fiihaa tusammaa Salsabiilaa.

١٨- عَيْنًا فِيهَا تُسَمَّىٰ سَلْسَبِيلًا ○

14. And the shades of the (Garden) Will come low over them, And the bunches (of fruit), there, Will hang low in humility.

15. And amongst them will bepassed round Vessels of silver and globets of crystal

16. Crystal-clear, made of silver: They will determine the measure thereof (According to their wishes).

17. And they will be given to drink there Of a Cup (of Wine) mixed with *Zanjabil*, -

18. A fountain there, called Salsabil.

19. Wa yatuufu `alay-him wildaanum-mukhalladuun: idhaa ra-'aytahum hasibtahum lu'-lu-'am-manthuuraa.

١٩- وَيَطُوفُ عَلَيْهِمْ وِلْدَانٌ مُّخَلَّدُونَ
إِذَا رَأَيْتَهُمْ
حَسِبْتَهُمْ لُؤْلُؤًا مَّنثُورًا ○

20. Wa idhaa ra-'ayta thamma ra-'ayta Na-`iimanw-wa Mul-kan-Kabiiraa.

٢٠- وَإِذَا رَأَيْتَ ثَمَّ رَأَيْتَ
نَعِيمًا وَّمُلْكًا كَبِيرًا ○

21. `Aaliyahum thiyaabu sundu-sin khudrunw-wa 'is-tabraq, wa hulluuu asaawira min-fid-dah; wa saaqaahum Rabbuhum Sharaaban-Tahuuraa.

٢١- عَالِيَهُمْ ثِيَابُ سُندُسٍ خُضْرٌ وَّ
إِسْتَبْرَقٌ
وَحُلُّوا أَسَاوِرَ مِن فِضَّةٍ
وَسَقَاهُمْ رَبُّهُمْ
شَرَابًا طَهُورًا ○

22. Inna haadhaa kaana lakum jazaaa-'anw-wa kaana sa`-yu-kum-mash-kuuraa.

٢٢- إِنَّ هَٰذَا كَانَ لَكُمْ جَزَاءً
وَّكَانَ سَعْيُكُم مَّشْكُورًا ○

19. And round about them Will (serve) Youths of perpetual (freshness): If you see them, You would think them Scattered Pearls.

20. And when you look, It is there you will see a Bliss and A Realm Magnificent.

21. Upon them will be Green Garments of fine silk And heavy brocade, And they will be adorned With Braclets of silver; And their Lord will give to them drink Of a Wine Pure and Holy.

22. " Verily this is a Reward For you, and your Endeavor Is accepted and recognized."

23. Innaa Nahnu nazzalnaa `alay-kal-Qur-'aana tanziilaa.

۲۳- إِنَّا نَحْنُ نَزَّلْنَا عَلَيْكَ الْقُرْآنَ تَنْزِيلًا ۝

24. Fas-bir li-Hukmi Rabbika wa laa tuti` minhum aathiman aw kafuuraa.

۲۴- فَاصْبِرْ لِحُكْمِ رَبِّكَ وَلَا تُطِعْ مِنْهُمْ آثِمًا أَوْ كَفُورًا ۝

25. Wadh-kurisma Rabbika bukratanw-wa 'asiilaa:

۲۵- وَاذْكُرِ اسْمَ رَبِّكَ بُكْرَةً وَأَصِيلًا ۝

26. Wa minal-lay-li fas-jud lahuu wa sabbih-hu lay-lan tawiilaa.

۲۶- وَمِنَ اللَّيْلِ فَاسْجُدْ لَهُ وَسَبِّحْهُ لَيْلًا طَوِيلًا ۝

27. Inna haaa-'ulaaa-'i yuhib-buunal-`aajilata wa yadharuuna waraaa-'ahum Yawman-thaqii-laa.

۲۷- إِنَّ هَٰؤُلَاءِ يُحِبُّونَ الْعَاجِلَةَ وَيَذَرُونَ وَرَاءَهُمْ يَوْمًا ثَقِيلًا ۝

23. It is We Who have sent down the Qur'an To you by stages.

24. Therefore be patient With constancy to the command Of your Lord, and hearken not To the sinner or the ingrate among them.

25. And celebrate the name of your Lord morning and evening,

26. And part of the night, Prostrate yourself to Him And glorify Him a long night through.

27. As to these, they love the fleeting life, And put away behind them A Day (that will be) hard.

28. Nahnu khalaq-naahum wa shadadnaaa asrahum; wa 'idhaa shi'-naa baddalnaaa amthaala-hum tabdiilaa.

٢٨- نَحْنُ خَلَقْنٰهُمْ وَ شَدَدْنَآ اَسْرَهُمْ ۚ وَ اِذَا شِئْنَا بَدَّلْنَآ اَمْثَالَهُمْ تَبْدِيْلًا ○

29. Inna haadhihii tadh-kirah: faman-shaaa-'attakhadha 'ilaa Rabbihii sabiilaa.

٢٩- اِنَّ هٰذِهٖ تَذْكِرَةٌ ۚ فَمَنْ شَآءَ اتَّخَذَ اِلٰى رَبِّهٖ سَبِيْلًا ○

30. Wa maa tashaaa-'uuna 'illaaa 'any-yashaaa - Allaah; innallaaha kaana `Aliiman Hakiimaa.

٣٠- وَ مَا تَشَآءُوْنَ اِلَّآ اَنْ يَّشَآءَ اللّٰهُ ؕ اِنَّ اللّٰهَ كَانَ عَلِيْمًا حَكِيْمًا ○

31. Yud-khilu many-ya-shaaa-'u fii Rahmatih; waz-zaalimiina a-`adda lahum `adhaaban aliimaa.

٣١- يُّدْخِلُ مَنْ يَّشَآءُ فِيْ رَحْمَتِهٖ ؕ وَ الظّٰلِمِيْنَ اَعَدَّ لَهُمْ عَذَابًا اَلِيْمًا ○

28. It is We Who created them, and We have madetheir joints strong; But, when We will, We can substitute The like of them by a complete change.

29. This is an admonition:Whosoever will, let him take a (straight) Path to his Lord.

30. But you will not, except as Allah wills; For Allah is Full of knowledge and wisdom.

31. He will admit to His Mercy Whom He will; But the Wrongdoers - for them has He prepared A grievous Penalty.

سُورَةُ المُرسَلات

Al Mursalāt

جزء 29

Bismillaahir - Rahmaanir - Rahiim. بِسْمِ اللّٰهِ الرَّحْمٰنِ الرَّحِيْمِ

1. Wal-MURASAALATI `urfaa, ١- وَالْمُرْسَلٰتِ عُرْفًا ۙ

2. Fal-`aasifaati `asfaa, ٢- فَالْعٰصِفٰتِ عَصْفًا ۙ

3. Wan-naashiraati nashraa, ٣- وَّالنّٰشِرٰتِ نَشْرًا ۙ

4. Fal-faariqaati farqaa, ٤- فَالْفٰرِقٰتِ فَرْقًا ۙ

5. Fal-mul-qiyaati dhikraa, ٥- فَالْمُلْقِيٰتِ ذِكْرًا ۙ

6. 'Udhran 'aw nudhraa; ٦- عُذْرًا اَوْ نُذْرًا ۙ

In the name of Allah, Most Gracious, Most Merciful.

1. By the (Winds) Sent Forth one after another (To man's profit);

2. Which then blow violently in tempestuous Gusts,

3. And scatter (things) Far and wide,

4. Then separate them, one from another,

5. Then spread abroad a Message,

6. Whether of Justification Or of Warning;

7. Innamaa tuu-`aduuna la-waaqi`.	٧-إِنَّمَا تُوعَدُونَ لَوَاقِعٌ ۝
8. Fa-idhan-nujuumu tumisat;	٨-فَإِذَا النُّجُومُ طُمِسَتْ ۝
9. Wa idhas-samaaa-'u furijat;	٩-وَإِذَا السَّمَاءُ فُرِجَتْ ۝
10. Wa idhal-jibaalu nusifat;	١٠-وَإِذَا الْجِبَالُ نُسِفَتْ ۝
11. Wa idhar-rusulu 'uqqitat;	١١-وَإِذَا الرُّسُلُ أُقِّتَتْ ۝
12. Li-ayyi Yawmin ujjilat ?	١٢-لِأَيِّ يَوْمٍ أُجِّلَتْ ۝
13. Li-Yawmil-Fasl.	١٣-لِيَوْمِ الْفَصْلِ ۝

7. Assuredly, what you are Promised must come to pass.

8. Then when the stars become dim:

9. When the heaven is cleft asunder;

10. When the mountains are Scattered (to the winds) as dust

11. And when the Messengers are (all) appointed a time (To collect);

12. For what Day are these (portents) deferred ?

13. For the Day of Sorting out.

۱۴- وَمَآ اَدْرٰىكَ مَا يَوْمُ الْفَصْلِ ۝

14. Wa maaa adraaka maa Yawmul--Fasl.

۱۵- وَيْلٌ يَّوْمَئِذٍ لِّلْمُكَذِّبِيْنَ ۝

15. Way-luny-Yawma-'idhil-lil-mukadh-dhibiin !

۱۶- اَلَمْ نُهْلِكِ الْاَوَّلِيْنَ ۝

16. Alam nuh-likil-awwaliin ?

۱۷- ثُمَّ نُتْبِعُهُمُ الْاٰخِرِيْنَ ۝

17. Thumma nutbi-`uhumul-'aa-khiriin.

۱۸- كَذٰلِكَ نَفْعَلُ بِالْمُجْرِمِيْنَ ۝

18. Kadhaalika naf-`alu bil-muj-rimiin.

۱۹- وَيْلٌ يَّوْمَئِذٍ لِّلْمُكَذِّبِيْنَ ۝

19. Way-luny-Yawma-'idhil-lil-mukadh-dhibiin !

14. And what will explain to you what is The Day of Sorting out ?

15. Ah woe, that Day, to the Rejecters of Truth ?

16. Did We not destroy the men of old (For their evil) ?

17. So shall We make Later (generations) Follow them.

18. Thus do we deal with men of sin

19. Ah woe, that Day. To the Rejecters of Truth !

20. Alam na<u>kh</u>-luq-kum-mim-maaa-'im-mahiin ?

٢٠-أَلَمْ نَخْلُقكُّم
مِّن مَّآءٍ مَّهِينٍ ○

21. Faja-`alnaahu fii qaraarim-makiin,

٢١-فَجَعَلْنَٰهُ فِى قَرَارٍ مَّكِينٍ ○

22. Ilaa qadarim-ma`-luum ?

٢٢-إِلَىٰ قَدَرٍ مَّعْلُومٍ ○

23. Faqadarnaa fani`-mal-Qaadiruun.

٢٣-فَقَدَرْنَا
فَنِعْمَ الْقَٰدِرُونَ ○

24. Way-luny-Yawma-'i<u>dh</u>il-lil-muka<u>dh</u>-<u>dh</u>ibiin !

٢٤-وَيْلٌ يَوْمَئِذٍ لِّلْمُكَذِّبِينَ ○

25. Alam naj-'alil-'arda kifaa-taa

٢٥-أَلَمْ نَجْعَلِ الْأَرْضَ كِفَاتًا ○

26. Ah-yaaa-'anw-wa 'amwaa-taa.

٢٦-أَحْيَآءً وَأَمْوَٰتًا ○

20. Have We not created you from a fluid (Held) despicable?

21. The which We placed In a place of rest, Firmly fixed,

22. For a period (of gestation) Determined (according to need) ?

23. For We do determine (According to need) ; for We Are the best to determine (things) !

24. Ah woe, that Day, to the Rejecters of Truth !

25. Have We not made the earth (as a place) To draw together

26. The living and the dead,

27. Wa ja-'alnaa fiihaa rawaa-
si-ya shaami-khaatinw-wa as-
qaynaakum-maaa-'an-furaataa ?

٢٧- وَّجَعَلْنَا فِيهَا رَوَاسِيَ شٰمِخٰتٍ
وَّأَسْقَيْنٰكُم مَّآءً فُرَاتًا ۝

28. Way-lun-Yawma-idhil-lil-
mukadh-dhibiin !

٢٨- وَيْلٌ يَّوْمَئِذٍ لِّلْمُكَذِّبِيْنَ ۝

29. Intaliquuu ilaa maa kun-
tum-bihii tukadh-dhibuun:

٢٩- اِنْطَلِقُوْٓا اِلٰى
مَا كُنْتُمْ بِهٖ تُكَذِّبُوْنَ ۝

30. Intaliquuu ilaa zillin-dhii
thalaathi shu-`ab,

٣٠- اِنْطَلِقُوْٓا اِلٰى ظِلٍّ ذِيْ ثَلٰثِ شُعَبٍ ۝

31. Laa zaliilinw-wa laa yughnii
minal-lahab.

٣١- لَّا ظَلِيْلٍ
وَّلَا يُغْنِيْ مِنَ اللَّهَبِ ۝

27. And made therein mountains standing firm Lofty (in stature) And provided for you Water sweet (and wholesome) ?

28. Ah woe, that Day To the Rejecters of Truth !

29. (It will be said:)" Depart you to that Which you used to reject as false !

30. " Depart you to a Shadow (of smoke ascending) in three columns,

31. " (Which yields) no shadow Of coolness, and is of no use against The fierce Blaze.

32. Innahaa tarmii bi-shararin-kal-qasr,

٣٢- إِنَّهَا تَرْمِي بِشَرَرٍ كَالْقَصْرِ ۚ

33. Ka-'annahuu jimaalatun-sufr.

٣٣- كَأَنَّهُ جِمٰلَتٌ صُفْرٌ ۗ

34. Way-lun-Yawma-'idhil-lil-mukadh-dhibiin !

٣٤- وَيْلٌ يَوْمَئِذٍ لِّلْمُكَذِّبِينَ ○

35. Haadhaa Yawmu laa yan-tiquun,

٣٥- هٰذَا يَوْمُ لَا يَنطِقُونَ ۙ

36. Wa laa yu'-dhanu lahum fa-ya`-tadhiruun.

٣٦- وَلَا يُؤْذَنُ لَهُمْ فَيَعْتَذِرُونَ ○

37. Way-lun-Yawma-'idhil-lil-mukadh-dhibiin !

٣٧- وَيْلٌ يَوْمَئِذٍ لِّلْمُكَذِّبِينَ ○

32. " Indeed it throws about Sparks (huge) as Forts,

33. " As if there were (a string of) yellow camels (marching swiftly)."

34. Ah woe, that Day, to the Rejecters of Truth !

35. That will be a day When they shall not Be able to speak,

36. Nor will it be open to them To put forth pleas.

37. Ah woe, that Day, To the Rejecters of Truth !

38. Haadhaa Yawmul-Fasl !
Jama`-naakum wal-aw-waliin !

٣٨-هٰذَا يَوْمُ الْفَصْلِ ۚ جَمَعْنٰكُمْ وَالْأَوَّلِيْنَ ○

39. Fa-'in-kaana lakum kay-
dun-fa-kiiduun !

٣٩-فَإِنْ كَانَ لَكُمْ كَيْدٌ فَكِيْدُوْنِ ○

40. Way-lun-Yawma-'idhil-lil-
mukadh-dhibiin !

٤٠-وَيْلٌ يَّوْمَئِذٍ لِّلْمُكَذِّبِيْنَ ○

41. Innal-Muttaqiina fii zilaa-
linw-wa `uyuun,

٤١-إِنَّ الْمُتَّقِيْنَ فِيْ ظِلٰلٍ وَّعُيُوْنٍ ○

42. Wa fawaakiha mimmaa
yashtahuun,

٤٢-وَّفَوَاكِهَ مِمَّا يَشْتَهُوْنَ ○

38. That will be a day Of sorting out ! We shall Gather you together And those before (you) !

39. Now, if you have a trick (or plot), Use it against Me !

40. Ah woe, that Day, To the Rejecters of Truth !

41. As to the Righteous they shall be amidst (Cool) shades and springs (of water),

42. And (they shall have) Fruits, - all they desire.

٤٣-كُلُوا وَاشْرَبُوا هَنِيٓـًٔا
بِمَا كُنتُمْ تَعْمَلُونَ ○

43. Kuluu wa<u>sh</u>-rabuu haniii-
'am-bimaa kuntum ta`-maluun.

٤٤- إِنَّا كَذَٰلِكَ نَجْزِي الْمُحْسِنِينَ ○

44. Innaa ka<u>dh</u>aalika najzil-
Muhsi-niin.

٤٥-وَيْلٌ يَوْمَئِذٍ لِّلْمُكَذِّبِينَ ○

45. Way-luny-Yawma-'i<u>dh</u>il-lil-
Muka<u>dh</u>-<u>dh</u>ibiin !

٤٦-كُلُوا وَتَمَتَّعُوا قَلِيلًا
إِنَّكُم مُّجْرِمُونَ ○

46. Kuluu wa tamatta-`uu qalii-
lan innakum-mujrimuun.

43. " Eat you and drink you To your heart's content: For that you worked (righteousness)."

44. Thus do We certainly Reward the Doers of Good.

45. Ah woe, that Day, to the Rejecters of Truth !

46. (O you Unjust !) Eat you and enjoy yourselves (But) a little while, For that you are Sinners.

47. Way-luny-Yawma-'idhil-lil-Mukadh-dhibiin !

٤٧-وَيْلٌ يَّوْمَئِذٍ لِّلْمُكَذِّبِيْنَ ۝

48. Wa idhaa qiila lahumur-ka-`uu laa yarka-`uun.

٤٨-وَاِذَا قِيْلَ لَهُمُ ارْكَعُوْا لَا يَرْكَعُوْنَ ۝

49. Way-luny-Yawma-'idhil-lil-Mukadh-dhibiin !

٤٩-وَيْلٌ يَّوْمَئِذٍ لِّلْمُكَذِّبِيْنَ ۝

50. Fabi-'ayyi Hadiithim-ba`-da-huu yu'-minuun ?

٥٠-فَبِاَيِّ حَدِيْثٍۢ بَعْدَهٗ يُؤْمِنُوْنَ ۝

47. Ah woe, that Day, To the Rejecters of Truth !

48. And when it is said to them, " Prostrate yourselves ! " they do not so.

49. Ah woe, that Day, To the Rejecters of Truth !

50. Then what Message: After that, Will they believe in ?